"Cooking is a true labor of love and Tara embodies that love in everything she does. This is a great glimpse into the world of cookery from a unique and playful perspective, one that is truly personal. A great guide, culinary tool, or simply a fun read!"

CHEF CRISTA LUEDTKE,
OWNER AND VISIONARY OF BOON BRAND

"Chef Tara is an innovative culinary professional with passion for flavor, creativity, and commitment to her craft."

CHEF SEAN ANDRADE,
CERTIFIED MASTER CHEF/CEO AWG
PRIVATE CHEFS

"Chef Tara's enthusiasm for cooking shows not only through her epic spice blend line, which we featured on *The Today Show*, but also in *The Journal of a Personal Chef,* where she shares a bit of inspiration for any amateur cook. Whether life is too busy, weekly menus have become monotonous, or mainstream cookbooks are too daunting, this is the text for you, chock-full of meal ideas, quick tips, and an unrivaled simplicity that brings things back to the basics."

JOEY SKLADANY,
FOOD WRITER AND
AUTHOR OF *BASIC BITCHEN*

"As a friend of Chef Tara's for two decades, I find her approach to writing inspiring and refreshingly brilliant! *The Journal of a Personal Chef: The First 52 Weeks* is so much more than a collection of ideas-this book provides inspiration and encouragement to try some fresh new dishes while leaving room for personalization. *The Journal of a Personal Chef* will inspire you to explore, experiment, and find joy in the kitchen!"

"Food has a way of bringing people together, and no one knows that better than Tara. As a lifelong friend and an incredible chef, Tara has spent years perfecting dishes that are as comforting as they are inspiring. This cookbook is a collection of her most cherished ideas—ones that have been shared over memorable conversations with family and friends.

With a mix of classic flavors, innovative twists, and personal stories woven throughout *The Journal of a Personal Chef* is more than just a book of ideas—it's an invitation to cook with heart, savor every bite, and make new memories around the table. Whether you're a seasoned home cook or just starting to experiment in the kitchen, these dishes will soon become staples in your kitchen. Grab an apron and get ready to cook like a chef!"

"For a full year, Chef Tara chronicled her life in the kitchen using her Moleskine journal—crafting weekly menus for a family of four without measurements, rigid recipes, or rules. Instead, she embraced the art of intuitive cooking, guiding readers through meals that are as approachable as delicious.

But this is more than just a culinary journal. Tara weaves an intimate journey—drawing from her days as a competitive athlete, her time in the corporate world, and ultimately discovering her true passion in the kitchen. Woven into the menus are personal anecdotes, industry insights, and the heartwarming moments that come with cooking for others. Whether you're an aspiring personal chef, a home cook seeking inspiration, or a foodie fascinated by the behind-the-scenes life of a chef, *The Journal of a Personal Chef* offers a fresh, joyful perspective on cooking.

As Picasso once said, "Learn the rules like a pro, so you can break them like an artist." And that's exactly what *The Journal of a Personal Chef* will invite you to do."

SILVIA VASQUEZ-LAVADO,
FOUNDER/CEO OF COURAGEOUS GIRLS,
AUTHOR OF *IN THE SHADOW OF THE MOUNTAIN*

FOR MOM.....Goodnight Moon

THE JOURNAL OF A PERSONAL CHEF

The First 52 Weeks

Ideas and Musings from the Kitchen

Tara Triefenbach

THE JOURNAL OF A PERSONAL CHEF
The First 52 Weeks: Ideas and Musings from the Kitchen
by Tara Triefenbach

CKB101000 COOKING/Courses & Dishes/General
CKB023000 COOKING/Methods/General
CKB131000 COOKING/Essays & Narratives

ISBN (paperback): 979-8-88636-051-6
ISBN (ebook): 979-8-88636-052-3
Library of Congress Control Number: 2025901225

Cover design by Lewis Agrell
All photos by Tara Triefenbach
Original Bird logo and Spice mix label designed by Michelle Maurer

Printed in the United States of America

Authority Publishing
13389 Folsom Blvd 300-256
Folsom, CA 95630
800-877-1097
www.AuthorityPublishing.com

AUTHOR'S NOTE

This book details the life of a personal chef over the course of one year—fifty-two weeks—providing weekly menus that were created to feed a family of four. This book is for anyone interested in new ideas to formulate weekly menus, finding new dishes that are family friendly, and discovering how easy it can be to make great food daily. It is also a daily encouragement to explore and play with food. Expand your horizons and get creative.

"The quiet stillness
of an empty kitchen
is a thing of peacefulness.
Becoming one with the food,
the knife an extension of my arm, hand, heart, and soul.
The first one in the kitchen,
6:15 a.m. turning the lights on,
hearing the slow hum as the ovens begin to heat.
Preparing a list of things to do today:
for today,
for tomorrow,
for the next day,
and the next.
Finding the rhythm of the kitchen
as tasks are completed." – Tara Triefenbach May 2, 2023

"Your simplicity is on a level of exquisite." This quote hangs on my refrigerator handwritten on a piece of yellow steno paper and it's from a friend that said this to me one Thanksgiving whilst I was preparing a feast for family and friends. It still rings true today as I cook with an ease about the kitchen that may be foreign to some. My goal for you is to help you get more comfortable in your own kitchen, to understand the simplicity of cooking, and to make your life easier by following the ingredients.

The quotes headlining each chapter were overheard throughout the kitchen on any given day and provided much laughter to us all at the house.

CONTENTS

CHAPTER 1

MEET THE CHEF

"What good is work if you can't have fun?"

BACK IN THE DAY, I WAS A COLLEGE VOLLEYBALL player by accident. I had been an athlete my whole life in a multitude of sports. I think I picked up a tennis racket first, then it was on to soccer, where I took on the mantle of goalkeeper. I loved soccer immensely and it quickly became my favorite sport. When my Seester (Seester is the term of endearment my sister Marnie and I use for each other) was old enough to play, Mom and Dad coached her team, so we were one big soccer family. Unfortunately, there wasn't high school soccer for girls in the 1980s where I grew up in Belleville, IL. I ended up switching to basketball and volleyball. I had played basketball most of my life as well, as Dad was a state championship winning coach and we had a half-court in our driveway. I really wanted to play basketball in college but alas, I got a volleyball scholarship, so that's what I ended up playing, and I am so grateful because those teammates of mine became my lifelong "people." But things would have looked a lot different had I been able to play soccer. Would I still be writing this book?

Volleyball it was, and I got my BA in marketing at the University of St. Francis in Joliet, IL. From there, I headed west to the University of San Francisco, where I got my master's degree in—you guessed it—sports marketing. I was the jock and nerd all in one, so it was a perfect fit. My first gig was at PowerBar in Berkeley, CA, and boy was that a fun gig. As marketing directors, we each had our own niche of what we focused on, and I had volleyball and water sports. Each weekend, we headed out of the office to various sporting events all over the country, promoting our signed athletes, sponsoring events, giving samples of PowerBars, and living the dream.

Following that amazing adventure, I jumped into another one working with JR Productions in Corte Madera, CA. We worked with indie singer-songwriters, promoting them, setting up gigs, and finding new up-and-comers in the music industry. That led my boss Jeanne and I to our work with The Breast Cancer Fund in San Francisco and partnering with the Lilith Fair Tour in 1998 with Sarah McLachlan. We oversaw the non-profit arm of the tour, traveling to fifty-seven shows in seventy-two days across the United States and Canada. All the money we raised that summer went to The Breast Cancer Fund and the amazing work they were doing.

Once I got off the road, I settled in San Francisco and went to work in sales at Veritas Software company in Silicon Valley. I spent nine years there and when it began to merge with Symantec, I started realizing that I didn't want to sit behind a desk forever. I knew it was time to follow my true passion: cooking.

Leaving behind my beloved San Francisco, where I had lived for two decades, I moved to Portland, OR, to enroll at Le Cordon Bleu, inspired by the culinary legend Julia Child. While Julia's journey took her to Paris, mine led me to the other "P"—Portland—but the excitement was the same.

Under the guidance of some of the most talented chefs, many of whom I still call friends, I found my true calling in the kitchen. It was there that I finally discovered what brought me happiness and peace: the art of cooking.

Most of my life I was not allowed in the kitchen. That was my mom's domain. I definitely did not get my desire to cook from Mom. We had dinner every night as a family; Mom, Dad, Marnie, and I, but it wasn't anything glamorous or gourmet. I remember lots of casseroles. It's also when I realized I hated sauerkraut. Mom would make this meal of mashed potatoes, white beans, and sauerkraut, and my dad loved it. I sat to Dad's right and I just remember the horrible odor that emanated off his plate as he piled it all up together. The most colorless meal ever and I held my nose when it was served.

We had dinner every night as a family. I say that again because that became the bedrock of all the things I try to accomplish with my cooking now for the families I work for. With much more color, of course.

I have so many hilarious stories from that dinner table. My Seester and I used to lean back on the back two legs of our chairs, daring each other to see who could lean back the furthest, as Mom warned us we'd fall back and crack our heads. Sure enough that happened, of course it did, and on one occasion there was a situation that involved a piece of bread covered in mustard that ended up all over the face of my Seester as the chair fell back to the ground.

No, I think I got my love of cooking from Grandma Walton, my mom's mom. She would make roast beef, mashed potatoes, gravy, and Amish noodles, and you would have thought we were eating a meal made for a king.

I got to make this meal with Grandma one last time before she passed, after I had gone to culinary school. I watched her make this masterpiece and to my amazement, I then realized as an adult that this roast beef was so well done there wasn't a speck of blood anywhere to be seen. It dawned on me then that grandma's well-done roast beef was so good and enjoyable because it was simply created from love.

If you love what you do, and do it with love, that will resonate through the dish.

Don't make it perfect. Make it fun and share the love. PLAY WITH FOOD!

The Call you Never Want to Get

In 2006 on a Wednesday, my Seester and I got a call from Mom saying Dad needed a quadruple heart bypass. And it was happening on Friday. We scrambled to get on a plane and make it there on time. It was incredibly hard to see my father in a surgical gown with tubes coming out of everywhere. He made it through the surgery just fine and it probably added twenty years to his life. It was also the scariest moment for all of us.

I was able to stay home for a few weeks and help Mom take care of Dad. Culinary school was about to begin so I had already started studying; I had a good feel for how to prepare healthy meals that Dad would eat. Remember how I wasn't allowed in the kitchen as a kid? Well, this was the turning point. I was finally able to convince Mom to relinquish control and let me take over and cook for Dad. I went from not washing the lettuce right to making dinner for my parents so that Dad could heal. He loved it because he was getting as much shrimp as he wanted.

The reverse happened when Mom was diagnosed with stage 4 pancreatic cancer on December 14, 2017. I moved home for those four months we had from diagnosis to her death on April 14, 2018, to help Dad take care of Mom. So once again, I played the role of nourisher for my parents, a role I took great pride in. I was making gourmet meals for three every night. I was making her favorite things for breakfast, lunch, and dinner.

The only problem is, with pancreatic cancer, Mom had ZERO appetite. Like, ZERO. She ate her Cheerios and broccoli cheddar soup, which we had to buy until I replicated it.

It was incredibly frustrating for me at first because here I was, making all this food that wasn't being appreciated the way it should have been. I learned a HUGE lesson in those months. No matter what I made, I couldn't expect everyone to eat it nor like it. Some things will be thrown in the garbage uneaten.

And that had to be ok.

Patience.

Breathe.

IT'S JUST FOOD, which became my mantra.

The lesson in all this came down to the fact that if someone is sick and not hungry, they aren't going to eat no matter what it is. At the end of the day, it didn't matter how beautiful and delicious the meal was, there was something bigger and more deadly in control. Not me.

CHAPTER 2

BECOMING A SOUS CHEF

"This isn't work for me, this is my retirement."

MY FIRST FORAY IN THE KITCHEN WAS AT JAKE'S GRILL in Portland, OR, right across the street from my culinary school. I stumbled into this externship because of my St. Louis Cardinals baseball hat. I happened to be in one afternoon after class, having a glass of wine, when one of the managers noticed my hat and came over for a chat. He was also a huge Cardinals fan, so we hit it off right away. I was still wearing my chef coat from school and explained to him that I was looking for an externship. He got me in the door for an interview with the executive chef.

An externship is a way to experience and have exposure to a certain job or industry. It's when you go outside of culinary school to work in a real environment to practice and gain insight into the work involved on a day-to-day basis. Also, it's needed in order to graduate. In a nutshell, you bust your ass for ten to twelve hours a day doing anything and everything and not getting paid.

Trust me when I say the externship is anything but glamorous. My first day, I was sent to the basement into a back room with no windows to dice about eight cases of onions for eight hours. Then it was on to peeling about ten cases of potatoes. No, I am not kidding and no, this isn't like walking up the hill both ways in the snow to get to school. I got the grunt work straight away. All the menial chores that no one in their right mind wants to do but must be done and done right as each little dice of the onion is essential to the success of the restaurant. It's like picking thyme. Cases and cases of thyme with its itty-bitty leaves.

My externship lasted eight weeks and I worked in different stations each week over the course of that time. I started in Garde manger, working with cold food preparation and salads. Then it was on to the hot line, making the hot sandwiches, manning the fryer, working the grill, and then on the line at the sauté station.

One night during the rush whilst on the sauté line, I had my ass handed to me. Jake's Grill is one of the oldest and most famous restaurants in Portland, so every night is like a Friday or Saturday in that it is constantly slammed. At any one time you could get twenty orders coming in at once, if not more.

Orders kept coming and coming and I was firing as fast as the expo could call out the orders. Faster and faster they came. Drop this, drop that, fire the steak, fire the filet, drop ten burgers. I thought I had it until I didn't, and our head chef yelled, "GET OFF THE LINE!" Tail between my legs, drenched in sweat, hands burning, I walked off the line for the first time and vowed it would be the last. I would never again allow myself to utterly fail in that capacity again.

It's important to note that it isn't until you sit down about an hour later and stop the movement that you realize you have succeeded in burning your hands and forearms, perfect red burn lines up and down the tender white underside of your arms. Then and only then do you smell the burning. Not of the food, but of yourself.

Following my externship, I worked in another small restaurant before landing a fantastic job at Reed College. My first day in the kitchen, the immediate thing I noticed was that there was a FEMALE on the main line. A woman was in the kitchen, not just working the salad station. My only experience thus far had been with all men. She looked to be someone with influence. As I continued to look around, I noticed more women than men hustling about. And I smiled.

That female on the line ended up becoming a great mentor and friend to me. Kelly took me under her wing and showed me the ropes. And those other women hustling about? Well, Juanita, Amparo, Andrea, Angie, and Bonnie—yeah, they ran the show and became some of my favorite people. Leticia, well, her handwriting is tattooed on my arm, and it reads: *"Estoy Cocinando."* (I am cooking.)

Estoy Cocinando los zapatos de tu abuela. (I am cooking your grandmother's shoes.)

When I arrived in the kitchen at six a.m., the only other women in that early with me were three fabulous Hispanic dishwashers that all worked their asses off. Truth be told, the dishwashers in the back of the kitchen are the ones that keep the place running. They have a long, hot day, all day, every day. You can't serve food on dirty dishes.

Each morning, I would greet them when they came in with a hug and a loud, empathic, *"Estoy cocinando..."* Some days I was cooking their grandmother's shoes (*los zapatos de tu abuela*), other days maybe their grandfather's pants (*los pantalones de tu abuelo*). It was something silly each morning and made them all laugh. "Ohhhh, Taracita."

If I can make my dishwashers laugh at six a.m., then I must be doing something right.

That also became my intro into learning to speak Spanish. Amparo and Leticia would teach me something new to say for the next morning.

Not enough can be said about the work ethic of the Mexican coworkers I had next to me every day. I have never known people that work harder. We would not have a restaurant industry without them.

As I worked my way up to becoming global chef and then catering chef, these women became indispensable, and I adored them. Being the global chef was probably one of my favorite gigs. Because Reed College has such an international student population, there was a station dedicated to the global cuisines of different countries. My job was to provide lunch every day out of that station for about 250-300 people a day in a two-hour time frame. What made it fun was that I would pick a different country each week, a different dish from that country each day. I would meet with the students from that region and ask them a simple question: "What is your favorite meal that your grandmother made?" From there, I would do my research on each dish to get an understanding of what I was going for. Some of the students even came back into the kitchen that morning to help me prep it and get it ready for lunch.

When it came time for lunch, I would take everything I had prepped out to the station and serve the students myself. I had so much fun engaging with all of them and my station became very popular throughout the weeks. I always had a surprise for them, one day even flying in live crawfish from Louisiana for a real live crawfish boil. I had them crawling around the station until they were ever so gracefully dropped into the large pot of boiling water. Once cooked, they were splayed out on newspaper with the corn, andouille sausage, and potatoes, like you were down in New Orleans for that day.

The greatest compliment I ever received was when one of the students who had helped me prepare her specific dish told me quite simply, "This is better than my grandmother's." I knew in that moment I was doing something right, something I was meant to be doing.

After six years with Bon Appetit Food Management Company, which runs food service for Reed College and other facilities all over the country, I ended up taking a job that would get me back to the Bay Area and what I consider home. I had finally made it to sous chef at Stanford University.

There was a time when I thought becoming/being a sous chef was the end all, be all. That I had made it...and then my body had other ideas. One Friday night on the line, I developed excruciating pain in my right ankle. The pain continued through the weekend and because I was a collegiate athlete and have had injuries before, I did the RICE (no pun intended) method: Rest, Ice, Compression, Elevate.

By Monday morning, I could barely walk. I was sent to occupational health on campus, which began the journey that would end my "Professional Kitchen" career, unbeknownst to me.

I ended up being diagnosed with tarsal tunnel syndrome in my right ankle that required surgery. "Well, that went well," I said with sarcasm. After a year and a half in a walking boot with no pain relief at all, it was suggested to me that I might need a spinal nerve stimulator. So that's what I got. My new reality of living life with Chronic Regional Pain Syndrome (CRPS) had begun.

What is CRPS, you ask? Well, CRPS is a chronic pain condition that most often affects the arms, legs, hands, or feet. CRPS is also known as reflex sympathetic dystrophy, or causalgia.

CRPS usually develops in a limb after an injury (such as a broken bone) or surgery. The exact cause of CRPS is unknown.

"Spinal cord stimulation (SCS) is a proven, long-term, and effective therapy for managing chronic pain. SCS disrupts the pain signals traveling between the spinal cord and the brain. Stimulation is delivered by a neurostimulator, a device like a pacemaker, implanted under the skin. The impulses travel from the device to the spine over thin, insulated wires called leads. The leads deliver mild electrical impulses to an area near your spine." (Medtronic.com)

After four surgeries and going it alone through recovery, I was struggling mentally and physically. I was depressed and wasn't quite sure where or what direction my world was going in.

Finally, a friend came for a visit and said, "I think it's time for you to come home." Never in a million years did I ever think I would leave San Francisco. But I had been alone and in pain for those years, with no hope in sight.

I went to Frankfort, IL, for Thanksgiving to enjoy the holiday with my friend Stacey and her kiddos and to possibly scope out what moving back would look like, where I would live, etc. Stacey is one of my closest friends from college and her family is like a second home for me.

On the day before I flew back to San Francisco, Stacey and I were out running errands when we popped into a pet shop. "Let's just go look," she said, which never ends well. And when I walked in, there sat the most adorable little puppy that looked like an Ewok. Now, anyone that knows me knows I am a huge Star Wars fan. She sat there and just stared at me—and I stared back—and in that moment, I knew she was mine. There sat my own personal Ewok I didn't know I needed.

"Well, she's going to be Smalls."

"You can't name a dog Smalls!" Stacey said.

"Watch me."

The next day, Smalls and I jumped on a plane and headed back to San Francisco to begin the preparations of moving back to Illinois. To say she was a hit at the airport would be an understatement. Smalls was exactly what I needed and has been my constant emotional support and by my side since that very first day. She was just an eight-week-old Shorkie (Shih Tzu/Yorkie) when I got her and now, she's ten.

In June 2015, I moved back to Illinois and settled in Frankfort, a town I have been coming to for thirty years and where Stacey grew up. We spent many college weekends in Frankfort. I have college friends around the area, and it is only a four-hour drive down to my hometown of Belleville, IL, where Mom and Dad were.

As I settled into my new town, I began doing catering events here and there and began developing my spice mix, figuring out how to sell it commercially. Because I couldn't work in a commercial kitchen anymore, catering small events around town worked for my body. I could do four to five events a month, make enough money to get by, and still manage the pain level. I could go big for two to three days then rest for two days.

In 2021 when Stacey, the one that encouraged me to move back to Illinois, dropped the bomb on me that she bought a house in Phoenix, AZ, I was left with feelings of devastation and confusion. I literally began imagining where I could go next. I had nothing really tying me to Frankfort anymore if she was leaving. Or so I thought.

What if I moved to Phoenix as well?

What about Palm Springs?

I could go to Sonoma and be close to Jen, my dearest friend since we were about fourteen years old when she played volleyball on my cousin Beth's team. She would later join me at the University of St. Francis on the volleyball team where we would find our "Frannie Pack"—Holly, Deb, Janene, Kendall, Carri, Shannon, Jen, and I, but that's a whole other book.

I could go back to the Bay Area and be close to my Seester, brother-in-law, nieces, and my big chosen family I have there.

I did a Google search for the best gay cities (yes, I know San Francisco is number one). If I was moving anywhere again, I needed my gays.

And then I got the phone call that would change everything in an instant.

After just one week on the job with this amazing family as their personal and private chef, I called Stacey and said, "You can go, I'm going to be ok."

CHAPTER 3

THE LIFE OF A PERSONAL CHEF

"I didn't hide any food under my plate."

A PERSONAL CHEF IS A CULINARY PROFESSIONAL WHO prepares custom meals for individuals, families, or small groups, typically in the client's home. Unlike restaurant chefs or caterers, personal chefs tailor their services to the specific preferences, dietary needs, and schedules of their clients. They often plan menus, shop for ingredients, and cook meals either on-site or prepare them in advance for later consumption.

Key Characteristics of a Personal Chef:

- Custom Menus: A personal chef creates personalized menus based on the client's preferences, dietary restrictions, and nutritional goals
- On-Site Cooking: Many personal chefs cook directly in the client's home kitchen, allowing for a more personal and tailored experience
- Meal Prep and Storage: A personal chef often prepares meals in bulk and packages them for later consumption, leaving reheating instructions for the client

- Flexible Services: A personal chef may work on a one-time basis, weekly, or even daily, depending on the client's needs. They can also cater small gatherings or events
- Focus on Health and Lifestyle: Many clients seek a personal chef for specific dietary needs (e.g., gluten-free, keto, vegan), making the chef's understanding of nutrition and dietary trends important

Who Hires a Personal Chef?

- Busy professionals or families: Those who don't have time to cook but want healthy, home-cooked meals
- People with special dietary requirements: Individuals with allergies, medical conditions, or strict dietary preferences
- Athletes or health-conscious clients: Those seeking to optimize nutrition for performance or health
- Individuals or families hosting small events: Clients who want the convenience of a private dining experience in their home

Overall, a personal chef provides a highly customized and convenient culinary service, offering tailored meals that align with individual tastes and lifestyles.

Living in Frankfort, IL, has given me the opportunity to continue to play with food. It allows me to practice my flavor profile by catering to my client's needs, no matter what the cuisine. It's not exactly how I envisioned my chef career going, as long as it went. I just wanted to be in the kitchen every day.

HOW THIS ALL CAME ABOUT

Friday, April 23, 2021, was the day that changed the trajectory of my life forever and for the better.

At 8:18 a.m., I received a phone call from an unknown number. I don't answer the phone if a name isn't attached to it because I get a lot of spam calls, so it went to voicemail. The typical spam voicemail is about nine to fourteen seconds in length. This voicemail was fifty-three seconds. Curiosity got the best of me, so I listened to it. She was calling on behalf of her client that needed a personal chef in Frankfort!

"Hi Tara. I'm calling on behalf of a client. We found your website online and he is looking for a personal chef because his daughter has some food allergies and just for convenience, they would like someone to come into their house and possibly prepare meals. I wanted to see if that is something indeed you do and offer this service on a recurring basis. And find out your availability to sit down with the family and find out what their needs are. They are in Frankfort, IL."

I called her back immediately and enjoyed a fifteen-minute conversation. Her next task was to set up a conference call with her client. The call was set for Tuesday, April 27, 2021, at 4:00 p.m.

All that weekend leading up to the conference call, I did my due diligence, made notes, did research on FPIES (more on this soon), and created sample menus.

The client and I talked for about forty-five minutes on that initial call and we set up a meeting for that Friday at his house at 5:00 p.m. to meet him and his wife.

We talked about all things food and life and when he told me about the upcoming construction of the outdoor kitchen, I put my hand on his arm and said, "Oh, my God, I love you," to which I immediately looked at his wife and said, "It's ok, I'm gay."

"When can you start?"

"How's Monday?"

So, on May 3, 2021, I began a new culinary journey. Mentally, I was being challenged daily. It was a physical challenge I was up for and one that my body was able to do because I could schedule the preparing of the meals around times of rest. It was a pleasant exhaustion, if that makes sense. Pleasant in the sense that I was back in the kitchen and doing what makes me happy for a family I adored.

What is FPIES?

When I had the original conversation back on April 27, 2021, one of the things my new client and I discussed was the fact that his youngest daughter had FPIES, and this was one of the reasons they wanted a personal chef.

What is Food Protein-Induced Enterocolitis Syndrome (FPIES)?

FPIES is a rare food allergy that affects the gastrointestinal (GI) tract. Unlike most food allergies, symptoms of FPIES do not begin immediately after eating. Instead, it can take hours before severe symptoms begin.

The most common FPIES food triggers are cow's milk, soy, rice, and oats, but any food can cause FPIES symptoms. Typical symptoms of FPIES include severe vomiting, diarrhea, and dehydration two hours after eating. These symptoms can lead to other complications, including changes in blood pressure and body temperature, lethargy, and failure to thrive.

For most people, FPIES is not a life-long condition. In fact, many children outgrow the condition by age three.

As time went on, she was able to experiment with more and more food groups to figure out what would or would not trigger her.

On certain occasions, I needed to get creative and swap out certain things or omit a piece of the recipe. We had a whole folder at the house for fun swaps for eggs.

She still couldn't eat eggs, rice, or soy, but she could now tolerate flour products. Over time, every meal I cooked I was able to include the youngest daughter. We were finally at a place where dinner was

AQUAFABA

Did you know that Aquafaba, which is the liquid in a jar or can of chickpeas, can be a substitution for egg whites? It's the viscous water in which legume seeds have been cooked in. It will mimic the functional properties of egg whites in cooking. Fascinating.

family style and for all four of them. No more meals where the youngest felt left out. She got to eat what her mom, dad, and sister ate.

2024 UPDATE: I am happy to report that now, three years later, she has completely outgrown FPIES and is eating like a worry-free child!

Nutrition Facts
Servings: 60, **Serv. Size:** 1.2 (2.5g), Amount Per Serving:
Calories 0, **Total Fat** 0g (0% DV), Sat. Fat 0g (0% DV), *Trans* Fat 0g, **Cholest.** 0mg (0% DV), **Sodium** 350mg (15% DV), **Total Carb.** 0g (0% DV), Fiber 0g (0% DV), Total Sugars 0g (incl. 0g Added Sugars, 0% DV), **Protein** 0g, Vit. D (0% DV), Calcium (0% DV), Iron (0% DV), Potas. (0% DV).

INGREDIENTS: ONION POWDER, ONION SALT, GARLIC POWDER, GARLIC SALT, ITALIAN SEASONING, CAYENNE, PAPRIKA, SALT, PEPPER

8 60011 72360 8

WWW.COOKINGTARA.COM

CHEF TARA'S

SPICE MIX

NET WT. 4 OZ. (113.4 G)

DEAR FRIENDS,

THIS IS A HANDCRAFTED, SMALL-BATCH GAME CHANGER. IT IS FOR EVERYONE, EVERYWHERE, IN EVERY KITCHEN WHO HAS EVER QUESTIONED WHAT SPICES TO USE.

ENJOY!

Chef Tara

HOW TO MAKE
CHEF TARA'S CROUTONS

YOU NEED:
1 FRENCH BAGUETTE, CUBED
1/2 CUP - 3/4 CUP OLIVE OIL

PREPARE:
TOSS WITH SPICE MIX
BAKE AT 350° FOR
25-30 MINUTES

CHAPTER 4

THE SPICE MIX STORY:
Handcrafted in small batches

"Sometimes when you are learning to cook, it can get messy."

WHEN I FIRST MOVED BACK TO ILLINOIS AND SETTLED in Frankfort, a small town about forty minutes south of Chicago, I spent a lot of time with my friends from college who were all still there. I cooked a lot for Stacey and her kids at her mom's house.

One day I was making Caesar salad to go with my lasagna and mixed a spice mix that I then tossed with the cubed sourdough bread and olive oil to make some homemade croutons. The aroma that filled the kitchen soon attracted Brandon and Cade, followed closely by Alexis and Paige. The croutons were instantly grabbed off the hot cookie sheet by the boys faster than I could get it to the salad.

Over the next few years this became a regular request for dinner...my "croutons with salad." I knew I was on to something if I could get kids to eat salad—and request it!

Around 2017, while eating a freshly made crouton, Brandon looked at me and said, "You need to bottle this." I made a large batch that summer when I was home with my parents and my mom helped me bag the first batch into $5 bags. We made about sixty of them. I peddled the little bags around town and very quickly realized that I might have a great business idea because they sold out instantly. I began the search for the best jars and lids and sifters to use. The first person I called was another college pal, Brett, who worked for TRICOR Braun, a packaging company. Next, I needed to find a web designer to create the website and a cool label. The Mueller's in Chicago knew just the person. Michelle not only designed my website, but also all my labels and any graphics I needed. It was all beginning to take shape.

Over the course of three years, I tested and explored all my options. I studied how to launch a product. I made sure everything was perfect and ready to go. But when is anything perfect? I had to just let go and send it out to the world.

During the Covid pandemic in 2020, I launched Chef Tara's Spice Mix. It sold fast because everyone was at home cooking. Right time, right product.

BOTTLING THE SPICE

In order to sell the product across the internet and through a distributor, I had to bottle it in a commercial setting. In other words, it had to be done in a fully functioning kitchen, and not in my home.

Thankfully, three blocks from my house are two restaurants owned by a friend. So, I was able to use their kitchens after the restaurant closed for the night. Then Covid hit and no one could go into anything. Luckily, my friend Caroline was one of the managers, so she agreed to start bottling for me. I made the mix by hand in large orange buckets. Then I would get the buckets, jars, lids, sifters, and sealers all down to Caroline to bottle. She's got it down to such a science that she's still my partner-in-crime and does the bottling. Now that I can go back into the restaurant with her, I assist HER. She can get about three batches done in around an hour.

One batch = 3 cases = 36 jars.

I do small batches to ensure adequate mixing of the nine ingredients and usually only do three to four batches during one bottling session.

If I had a large processing plant, of course I could do mass production. But for now, it works. Once Caroline gets everything bottled, I bring the jars back home to get them labeled and ready to ship. I handle all the selling and shipping direct to the customer and to my original retail outlet, Eckert's Country Farm and Store, in my hometown of Belleville, IL. My high school friend Angie married into the Eckert family, so Angie was one of my first calls when this all started. To this day she has been one of my biggest supporters.

My mom loved Eckert's, but alas, she is missing out on some really cool things. She was the first one to help me bag the spice mix when I first created it. When Eckert's started carrying my spice mix, I wanted to call my mom and tell her. I remembered that I couldn't, and I cried tears of happiness and sadness. She would have been over the moon.

We started going to Eckert's as kids to pick apples, enjoy hay-rides, and to find the perfect Christmas tree. Eckert's is a part of my childhood, so to be selling in the store, well, Mom just wouldn't have believed it.

I can see her now at Eckert's, telling every customer in the store that her daughter is a chef and that they sold my spice mix there. She would have sold tons of jars. She was the original HYPE GIRL.

CHAPTER 5

THE ARGUMENT FOR NO QUANTITIES

"Oh, you even have all your signage on!"

"I don't follow recipes, I follow ingredients."
– Erin French, *The Lost Kitchen*

I STRUGGLE OFTEN WHEN SOMEONE ASKS ME FOR recipes. I can tell you what is in it, and I can tell you exactly how to make it, but when it comes to how much, I usually don't have a clue. I add until it looks good, tastes good, feels right. I pour this and that, dice, cut, mince, and add to the pot.

The components are there so play with it…try different options, test your palate, and remember, it's just food.

Full disclosure, I am not a baker. That would require measuring things. Get creative, make it your own, which is what I do every day. If I have an idea, I often do research, looking at four or five different recipes to make sure the ingredients I have in my mind are on the right track to what the dish should taste like. Expand your flavor profile, and taste everything often. I encourage you to do the same.

For most of these dishes, I can tell you where I was and when I had it. My favorite things, chefs, and restaurants all inspire me, so I look to them for ideas to feed a hungry household daily.

For most everything you want to make, the recipe is already out there in one form or another. I don't necessarily have to make up a new recipe for a dish every day. I need to be able to look at it, figure out the flavor profile, and make it happen. More often than not, I make slight alterations to the dish based on individual preferences.

I don't follow a recipe; I use it as an inspiration.

As I was putting this project together, Sam Sifton, the founding editor of NYT Cooking, came out with the *No-Recipe Recipes* cookbook. I instantly bought it and said, "This—this is what I am talking about!" I use the NYT Cooking app on the daily for much of my research.

In his book, Sifton discusses the laying out of strict instructions for how to best prepare specific dishes. "These recipes take a particular form: a list of ingredients and measurements that are followed by step-by-step directions for how to use them to result in a finished dish."

Sifton then goes on to say, "But I don't just cook with recipes, and I am not alone. Indeed, cooking without recipes is a kitchen skill, same as cutting vegetables into a dice or flipping an omelet. It's a proficiency to develop, a way to improve your confidence in the kitchen and makes the act of cooking fun, when it sometimes seems like a chore." (*No-Recipe Recipes*). This is my intent: to get you more confident with your ability to make a fabulous meal.

SEASON TO TASTE

What does season to taste mean? By definition, it means to add as much salt or pepper or as much of a spice or herb as one likes so something tastes good.

Makes sense, right? In my opinion, it means to add the seasonings and the amount that suits your taste buds. If you like it salty, then add more salt. If you like more pepper in it, then add it. If you love the taste of fresh basil, then add more basil. This is your dish, so add until you think the flavor is right.

This is when the practice of figuring out your flavor palate comes into play. Learning and studying flavor profiles of different ingredients from around the world is "playing with food."

There are two books that were indispensable to me throughout my studies. The first one, *The Flavor Thesaurus* by Niki Seguit, literally shows you what works with what in pairs.

"Following the instructions in a recipe is like parroting pre-formed sentences from a phrase book. Forming an understanding of how flavors work together, on the other hand, is like learning the language: it allows you to express yourself freely, to improvise, to find appropriate substitutions for ingredients, to cook a dish the way you fancy cooking it" (*The Flavor Thesaurus*).

Niki goes on to say, "I've assumed you know that you usually used to add salt to savory dishes, taste them, and adjust before you serve, turn off the stove when you're finished, and fish out any ingredients that might choke your loved ones" (*The Flavor Thesaurus*).

"If something in a recipe isn't clear, stop, think, and if the solution isn't forthcoming, find a similar recipe and see if that sheds light" (*The Flavor Thesaurus*).

This is what I hope you can take away from the book. Using the ideas and suggestions I have given you so that you can flesh out what the dish will ultimately become.

How exactly does chocolate pair with bacon? Does it really matter? It's delicious!

But you get the idea. Niki broke down ninety-nine essential flavors and created pairings for each. If you are a nerd like I am, grab that book and study flavor profiles to really enhance your cooking style.

The second great resource I use, *Culinary Artistry*, takes it a step further and examines the art of menu planning. It discusses how chefs select and pair ingredients, how flavors are combined into dishes, and how dishes become menus.

Since you don't necessarily need to create a menu, as I have done it for you, it is a great reference material if you ever want to know what to do with the carrot that you have left in your refrigerator. Or get creative and DO build your own weekly menus. Mix and match what I have shown you with something of your own. Try it!

THE BLACK BOX CHALLENGE

In culinary school, one of the final tests is the Black Box Challenge. We were given five ingredients, unknown to us prior to cooking, in a black box. We had to create an appetizer, a salad, a side dish, and an entrée—all in three hours.

I was one of the older students in our class at thirty-six years old, similar in age to many of my professors. I had created a nice relationship with them, some of whom are still friends of mine to this day. I can always call them to pick their brain.

Which is why I think they thought it was HILARIOUS to give me BEEF HEARTS as my protein. REALLY???

We were allowed to use anything in the pantry, so I knew one of the only ways I could prepare the beef hearts was to slow braise them in liquid. I grabbed beef stock and red wine (which I should have taken a shot of), and after a quick sauté and browning of the beef hearts, I put the pot in the oven, set the temp for 325 degrees, said a prayer to the Food Gods, and hoped for the best.

There was nothing I could do with that dish for the next two and a half to three hours, except pray it worked, so I got to work on the other components of my Black Box meal. I literally have no idea what else I made as it all became a flurry of action, plating, and a giant blur just hoping those beef hearts cooked properly.

Clearly, I passed, as I am here today and doing what I love, but again…really?

Think of this book/journal as your own personal mini Black Box Challenge!

You are given all the ingredients, now GO! Make it your own.

Share it with me, show me what you made.

Take pictures and tag me on social media @cheftaratree with the hashtag: #cheftarachallenge.

"Anyone can cook anything and make it delicious" (*SALT, FAT, ACID, HEAT*).

CHAPTER 6

MENU PLANNING LAYOUT

"Burpy Gonzalez over here."

FOR EACH WEEK, I HAVE PROVIDED FIVE MEALS BY the day that I cooked them. You don't have to follow my schedule; these are just ideas for you to start to look at your week all set up.

For each dish, sauce, or vinaigrette, I have given you the list of ingredients. I have tried to list them in the order that they should be added or used.

You will see some duplicates on the weekly menus because some dishes are dog-eared as family favorites.

I am not reinventing the wheel here. Ingredients are out there, recipes are out there, and I find inspiration from those that continue to amaze me daily. I research and research the best of the best to find new and exciting dishes for my clients. As I mentioned before, I will look at four or five different recipes to wrap my brain around what I am wanting to make. Then I make it my own, as I am encouraging you to do.

METHOD TO THE MADNESS

This book was developed from my Moleskine journal that I use every day. It may look a bit daunting, but there is a method to my madness.

1. DATE

2. WEEK NUMBER IN RED PEN

3. DINNER IDEAS IN RED PEN: I list out the ideas then assign a day of the week.

4. LUNCH IDEAS

5. GROCERY LIST: I try and list by dish to make sure I have everything I need to accomplish that dish.

6. FREEZER: Because we buy our own cow and pig, a lot of the proteins get pulled a few days in advance, as well as the salmon, cod, and halibut we get from Alaska.

7. SCHEDULE CHANGES: Any day of the week can change depending on work schedules or appointments.

8. DAILY TO-DO'S: Each day is broken down into a list of tasks that need to be completed. For any given dish, whether it's lunch or dinner, five to ten things need to be accomplished to get it to the table.

① 1/17/22   ② Week 38   ③   ④ 8   MON ⑧   ⑦ Thur — lunch B!
Ideas   NO No.

F. Minestrone 4/8   X Avo Toast   No Lunch   WED
Chx Stir Fry w/Rice   Soba Bowl   Parfaits x5.   Caesar
Steak brussels potatoes cottage cheese Taco Salad Omelet   X Cut chx
Taco Tuesday   X Chx Caesar   Protein Box x2   X make sauce
Seafood — Halibut Asparagus 1/1   Halibut X Salmon — MB X cook off rice
                                                Roast Asparagus   X noodles? yes
⑤   ⑥ Freezer   Miso Glaze
Ground Beef   X Yogurt   Ground Beef x2   X 1 t ginger
Tomato   Tortillas   Chx   X 2 t mirin   TA   yes
Lettuce — my garden Sourdough Steak x2   X 3 T miso   X NO LUNCH
Mex Cheese   X bean sprouts Ground Turkey   X Rice   X Make minestrone
Shells   Avocado   X lunch — chopped
Halibut   THE   X Harvest lettuce
Asparagus   Stone Valley Plain   X Avo Toast   Taco Salad?
Brussels   — whole milk   X Chx Breast Prep this brine Veg Wrap
Potato   X Rasp   Prep Veg   Chx apple salad
Rice — Ready   X Straw   X Zucc   X Oven @ 400
Zucchini   X Blues   X Spinach   X Bake Potatoes 4:5
Squash   X Avocado   X Sear Steak
Stock   X Bananas   X Peppers   X Roast brussels
Onion   Clementine Oranges   X Broccoli   Omelet
Lima bean-butter bean X Oranges   X Bok Choy   X Check Parfaits
peas   X Green Beans   X Onion   X Cook off Pasta
Bok Choy   X Broccoli   Harvest Romaine X Make Balsamic Vin
Carrots   Ground Turkey   Croutons
Peppers X red   Lunch W Caesar
     X sage   Fire chx breast
                                                Make caesar
                                                Dice Tomatoes Brown Beef
                                                Cut lettuce

CHAPTER 7

A DAY IN DETAIL

"Chef Tara, by your house was it a Stanley Steamer day?"

A TYPICAL WEEK STARTS DURING THE WEEKEND WITH menu planning and starting the grocery list. Once the list is set, shopping commences all before Monday morning at 10:30 a.m. I oftentimes used a personal shopper, who would go to two or three stores to make sure everything on the list was secured.

Saturday and Sunday: Menu plan, build grocery list

Monday, Tuesday, and Thursday:

8:30: Grocery list sent, and shopping begins (Monday only)

10:50: Groceries delivered (Monday only)

Arrive at the house

Unload groceries (Monday only)

Clean countertop

Mise en place: Get my cutting board out, grab my salt, pepper, and Chef Tara's Spice Mix containers, my box of disposable gloves, and my chef knife. A clean towel on hand, which is bound to get dirty. Always have open containers of salt and pepper (and for me, my original spice mix) by your cutting board so you can easily season your proteins and vegetables.

MISE EN PLACE

Mise en place is a French kitchen phrase that means "putting in place" or "gathering." It refers to the discipline and organization a good chef exhibits in the kitchen. To practice mise en place, a chef should have all their ingredients and supplies prepared and organized before they begin cooking.

Mise en Place Steps

- Step 1: Read over the entire recipe and develop a plan
- Step 2: Prioritize your work
- Step 3: Collect tools and prepare equipment
- Step 4: Gather recipe ingredients
- Step 5: Prepare and measure ingredients
- Step 6: Set up your workstation

11:00: Lunch prep

12:15: Lunch served

Begin dinner prep

Dice, cut, chop, make sauces, make vinaigrettes

1:45/2:00: Break, nap, eat lunch, feet up

5:00: Back to the kitchen

Finish dinner prep

Pull dishes and silverware

6:30: Plate and serve dinner

Clean up

7:00: Depart for home and Smalls and scrounge up something to eat. Fun fact: I rarely cook for myself. So, sometimes it's quick from the freezer to microwave butter chicken or a pizza. Or a sandwich from Jersey Mike's or Beijing beef from Panda Express. I have tried a meal delivery service that brings home-cooked meals to me and that worked for a while. It's not ideal, but I am so shattered at the end of the day, I just need substance in me. Sometimes a good bowl of cereal or granola and yogurt does the trick as well.

On Wednesday, I don't go in until 5:00 p.m., so on that day, I have everything already queued up and I just fire all the components for that evening's meal.

WHAT A FULL WEEK LOOKS LIKE

SUNDAY

Sunday, and some of Saturday as well, is spent doing research. I scour the cookbooks in my personal library, check and see what's going on in the NYT Cooking app, and read the emails in my inbox from cooking sites. I try and plan out one fish, one chicken, and one red meat dish per week. When I find a dish I like and want to replicate, I again do research and look up five or six different variations of the same dish. Then I take the ingredients and make it my own. As I have said before, I don't use recipes per se, to the letter or at all. I don't use quantities, I just do. I know most people love to have a recipe telling them exactly what to put in a dish. And that's great. But I am challenging you to get creative. I don't always have five lunches in my head set in stone, rather three or four planned and then see how the week goes. Then I use what I have on hand and allow for spontaneous ideas. Sometimes the client may come down that morning and say she is craving a grilled cheese and tomato soup. Well, I better have those components on hand! That changes the plan, and whatever I may have planned for lunch that day gets pushed out to the next day. After I have my five dinners set and lunch ideas planned out, I start to make the grocery list. Listing out all the components of every dish is essential, obviously. I may be making a salad one day, which also includes everything that goes into that salad, but also all the ingredients in the dressing I'll need to make as well. Don't forget all the individual components of that Asian slaw you are using on the street tacos. And the little sesame seeds you need for the garnish. Look at each dish and break it down into its individual pieces.

MONDAY

The To-Do List:

- Make croutons for the Caesar lunch salad
- Cook off one chicken breast for the salad and one for the lunch entree, which includes broccoli and sweet potatoes

- Prep broccoli by cutting into florets
- Dice the sweet potatoes
- Sauté together in olive oil
- Make the dressing for the Caesar salad
- After lunch is done, I make parfaits for the week for breakfast
- Because I am making risotto tonight for dinner, I need to prep the vegetables
- Slice mushrooms and asparagus
- For this meal, I am adding chicken to one serving of the risotto for extra protein

TUESDAY

Today's lunch is scallop ceviche for Mom and turkey burger with roast sweet potatoes and broccoli for Dad. This is a lot of prep to do, so having this list makes it easier. No chore is too small.

Today, I need to (in no particular order):

- Make the turkey burger into a patty and season liberally
- Dice cucumber
- Dice red pepper
- Dice onion
- Dice mango
- Add garlic and mint to create the ceviche
- Dice sweet potatoes
- Trim broccoli
- Pick dill and make a dill creme sauce

At the same time, I am cooking off chicken breast for Wednesday's BBQ chicken salads. While I am making the dill creme, I am also making a dill ranch dressing for Wednesday's salad.

I make the salads for Wednesday because I can't get into the kitchen until dinner time.

Dinner is at 6:30, so right when I arrive, I turn on the oven to preheat. Most mornings I can get dinner prep done, but Tuesday and Thursday I am doing double duty by making the lunches for

Wednesday and Friday. So, dinner prep doesn't happen until I get in at 5:00 p.m. and then I:

- Quarter potatoes
- Cut asparagus
- Toss with olive oil, salt, and pepper
- Prep salmon with olive oil, salt, and pepper
- Fire potatoes first as they will take about 40 minutes
- Then fire asparagus and salmon to cook for about 10 minutes

While everything is in the oven, I get the plates ready, silverware out, fruit cut for the littles, so all I need to do is put the hot food down.

> **Cooking Process**
>
> **When I use the term "fire," it means to start the actual cooking process—put it in the oven, start sautéing it—start making it hot. Prior to this step, make sure you have read and decided of what the ingredients entail. What needs to be prepped, cleaned or chopped? Have your seasonings at the ready. Figure out if you need to sauté, blanche, grill, roast or emulsify.**

WEDNESDAY

My day in the kitchen doesn't start until about 5:00 p.m.

On this Wednesday, we are having a house favorite, turkey lettuce wraps.

Since I wasn't there for the lunch session, I need to get all my mise en place done.

I immediately start browning the ground turkey, dicing the mushrooms and water chestnuts, then adding these to the turkey and continuing to cook through.

Then I make two sauces. One as a cooking sauce and the other as the dipping sauce. I use whole heads of bibb or butter lettuce, so at this point while the turkey is simmering, I wash, dry (I hate wet lettuce) and separate the leaves to make perfect little bowls arranged on a large white platter. Add the cooking sauce to the turkey mixture. Serve the dish by plating the turkey mix in the lettuce cups with the dipping sauce on the side in a white ramekin.

THURSDAY

Thursday is a bit like Tuesday in that I am doing multiple days at once. Not only do I get Thursday lunch and dinner ready, but I also do Friday's lunch and dinner.

White Platter

Try and use white platters, dishes, or plates when you can to present your food. It allows the colors of the food to shine so the consumer can really appreciate the food visually.

Here's how this morning goes using "all the things":

- Turn on the oven to preheat to 425 degrees
- Brown ground beef in two different pots
- In one pot, add taco spices
- In the other pot, start the beginning of chili
- In a third pot, start boiling water to cook off pasta for the chili mac
- Make tortilla bowls by baking them off in the oven
- Dice tomatoes
- Shred lettuce
- Strain black beans
- Make guacamole
- Add cheese and sour cream and finish the taco salads
- Prep chili add-ons and bowl up:

   o Diced onion
   o Shredded cheddar cheese
   o Sour cream
   o Oyster crackers

- Have an avocado ready but do not cut until use to prevent it from turning brown
- Finish the chili and into the crock pot it goes, but not turned on, for use over the weekend

It looks like I pulled an audible and changed up the menu, which is bound to happen with a busy family of four. BE FLEXIBLE!

Thursday night went from a caprese pasta to steak with mushrooms and sweet potatoes. I can guess that a meeting got canceled and the whole family ended up being there for dinner instead.

- Begin by turning on the grill
- Slice mushrooms
- Dice sweet potatoes
- Sauté together in olive oil, salt, and pepper
- Fire the steak, cook to medium rare, and slice against the grain
- Plate and serve

Again, be flexible. Plans could change instantly. You can't get offended if you just made a four-course meal, someone gets sick and a hospital visit happens. Not from the food, of course, rather a virus picked up at school, in the park, at work, or from life in general.

Or a meeting runs late.

Or someone throws up.

Or two more people are now coming to dinner.

CHAPTER 8

MY KITCHEN MUST-HAVES

"Don't blow your nose in your hand."

THESE ARE THINGS I CAN'T LIVE WITHOUT IN MY everyday work life as a personal chef. Full disclosure, I am not getting paid for listing any of the brands you see below, though if anyone wants to sponsor me, I will not say no. These are just my things, what I like and use and where I get them. I hate when I read in a book about someone's favorite thing, and they don't tell me where to find it to buy it! I need instant gratification. So, I will not leave you hanging. You can go get everything today!

Diamond Crystal salt: The best all-purpose salt in my opinion. You can get it at Gordon Food Service or most restaurant supply stores. Or Amazon, of course.

Chef Tara's Spice Mix: What can I say, I created this for one purpose, and it has evolved into a multi-purpose spice mix that I use on about ninety percent of everything I make in the kitchen. It has become the one spice mix that you need in your spice cabinet. Because I mention it in most ideas and you may not have it YET, I'll tell you what is in it: onion powder, onion salt, garlic powder, garlic salt, Italian seasoning, cayenne pepper, paprika, salt, and pepper. There are also five new varieties to try. https://www.cookingtara.com/

Pepper grinder: Williams-Sonoma makes one that I use in the kitchen.

Soy sauce: I use the organic Shoyu from Whole Foods, but Kikkoman makes a great one that is widely available at most grocery stores.

Hoisin sauce: Another Asian sauce I can't live without. It goes hand in hand with the soy, rice vinegar, and mirin in my everyday sauce. I use the organic version from Whole Foods, but Kikkoman, San J, and Lee Kum Kee make this sauce that is available in most grocery stores.

Mirin: This is a Japanese rice cooking wine I use in many of my sauces. I use the Eden Food's brand from Whole Foods, but again, Kikkoman and other brands make this, and it is available in your local grocery store.

Rice vinegar: This might be my favorite vinegar to use, closely followed by balsamic. It is versatile in Asian sauces as well as vinaigrettes, and even for the best mignonette to pair with your oysters. I can't live without rice vinegar in my kitchen. Marukan is the brand I use and is available in grocery stores.

"Unseasoned rice vinegar is the purest form of rice vinegar out there and doesn't contain any extra additives or flavors. For most, this is the default rice vinegar in the pantry. It's great for pickling or sauces. Flavored with a bit of salt and sugar, seasoned rice vinegar is terrific for salad dressings and marinades. This is also the vinegar to use if you're making sushi rice or want a quick pop of flavor without having to spend too much time in the kitchen." – Clarissa Wei for Food Network

Oyster sauce: Another must-have for most of my sauces. It adds that umami flavor, adding a richness and the savory I look for.

Toasted sesame oil: Essential for Asian vinaigrettes, a great tuna poke, and cooking for stir-fries. I use the Spectrum brand from Whole Foods for most of my oils and vinegars.

Extra virgin olive oil: You literally can't build a kitchen pantry without this.

Grapeseed oil: This is lighter than the extra virgin olive oil and has a higher smoke point, so I use it a lot when cooking with the wok. It's great in vinaigrettes as well. La Tourangelle is a brand I use.

Balsamic vinegar: I use two different versions of balsamic in my kitchen. One for everyday balsamic vinaigrette and marinades, and the other in a glaze form for my avocado toasts and finishing a caprese salad. I also keep on hand a white balsamic vinegar.

Ball jars: Just like Grandma used to use, though hers were mostly for pickling and canning/jarring tomatoes and fresh vegetables from the garden. I use mine for making and storing all my sauces, vinaigrettes, and dressings. They are also great for my parfaits and overnight oats for breakfast. The pint-size jars are perfect for a quick sauce that you are using that night. The quart-size jars are used for a vinaigrette or dressing I will store all week.

Ball jar reusable lids: Another huge essential are the Ball Jar reusable lids! These replace the metal lids that I have often found to get rusty after quite a few uses. These just go right in the dishwasher with the jars and are ready for another use. The best finds over the last few years.

T-Fal sauté pan: I know there are a lot of fancy pans out there, but this one is a work horse for me that I can beat up and not feel bad about it. The non-stick surface works perfectly and it's easy to clean. It's too affordable to pass up.

T-Fal wok: Another work horse of a pan, I found mine at Target in RED! Yes, I know there are so many amazing woks out there, and if anyone wants to find me an old school WOK used by someone's grandma from eons ago, I will gladly accept it. But, until then, I use this one weekly. It holds everything I need in the same pan and is easy to clean. I can beat it up, and it keeps doing the job.

Big pasta pot: We use All-Clad, but any big pasta pot works. I am not one to use a strainer inside the pasta pot while cooking is taking place. I think it just adds more time to the overall cook time of your food, and time is of the essence in my kitchen.

Le Creuset Dutch oven: One of my favorite things ever. I have had my blue four-quart one forever. Thankfully we have all things Le Creuset in the kitchen, so I have two different Dutch ovens I use on the regular. But go crazy and pick your style and color! I have the four-quart pot and there is a five-and-a-half-quart pot in the family's kitchen for all things soup.

Red tongs: You can no longer buy the specific ones I have. Mine are red, Kitchen-Aid, with the square silicone pads at the ends. I have had mine for probably fifteen years. Find yourself a good pair that you love and hold on to them. I almost lost mine once after a catering event, and I about lost my mind. These go with me everywhere.

Moleskine hard-cover journal: My Seester and I have been using Moleskine for as long as we can remember. It's our go-to trusty journal. My red Moleskine that I used for the first year in the kitchen with the family is what this book is based on. The kiddos have said that I must get all the Moleskine in the color of the rainbow and go in order. I have used four other Moleskines in the writing of this book for notes, drawings, and research. I love Moleskines and can't say enough great things.

Sharpie S-gel pens: Sharpies are just the best. Always. I use Sharpie markers for labeling and the pens for writing everything else in the Moleskine journal I keep daily with the menus. I use red ink for the menu ideas, blue or black ink for the grocery list, then whatever I didn't use for the grocery list gets used for my to-do lists each day. You need at least three colors of pens!

Apron: I have a fun denim apron that I love, but I have a Hedley and Bennett apron I had made with my name on it and the colors of the rainbow for the kiddos at the house.

Shun 10" chef knife: I love this knife so much it is literally tattooed on my left arm. This was my first "big girl knife" when I went off to culinary school, and it's the only knife I use on a consistent basis.

White cutting board: I have a large, white, plastic, restaurant grade cutting board from Gordon Food Service (GFS) that I can't cook without. In many kitchens, cutting boards are color coded based on what you are cutting. Red is for raw proteins, meats, and poultry; green is for fruits and vegetables; and blue is for seafood.

Disposable gloves: I never handle raw proteins without using gloves. Less contamination and I don't have to wash my hands 500 times a day. Find a good box at GFS or on Amazon that are vinyl, powder free, and latex free.

CHAPTER 9

WEEKLY MENUS 1-52

"If something is worth doing, it's worth OVER doing."

Week 1
Boeuf bourguignon over Amish noodles
Salmon with roasted Brussels sprouts and roasted potatoes
Baked ziti
Chicken and shrimp pad Thai
Chicken enchiladas

Week 2
Chicken lettuce wraps with soy dipping sauce
Cod fish tacos with mango salsa and guacamole
Meat lasagna with cream cheese, mozzarella, parmesan, and marinara served with garlic bread
Naan pizza three ways with pepperoni and pineapple, BBQ chicken, and margarita style
Shepherd's pie

Week 3
Steak stir-fry with seasonal vegetables
Scallops over fettuccine alfredo
Chicken parmigiana over spaghetti noodles

Breaded pork chops with grilled asparagus and roasted potatoes
Frittata with ham and cheddar cheese

Week 4
Smash burgers with sweet potato fries and mac and cheese
Miso glazed salmon with stir-fried vegetables over udon noodles
Roasted chicken with potatoes and baby carrots
Steak fajitas with red, orange, and green peppers, onions, and
guacamole
Pulled pork with creamy coleslaw and Mom's potato salad

Week 5
Coconut shrimp with seasonal vegetable stir-fry and cauliflower rice
Flank steak with chimichurri, roasted Brussels sprouts, and roasted
potatoes
Baked Ziti with penne pasta
Chicken satay with cucumber and onion salad
Chicken Enchiladas with cheese

Week 6
Mushroom risotto with peas and pancetta
Salmon with avocado salsa
Herb-roasted pork tenderloin with broccolini and au gratin potatoes
Shrimp stir-fry with seasonal vegetables
Chicken parmigiana over spaghetti noodles

Week 7
Slow braised Korean short rib tacos with Asian slaw and guacamole
Angel hair pasta with olive oil, asparagus, tomato, and basil
Mexican pot pie
Croque monsieur and French fries
Mushroom quiche

Week 8
Naan pizza three ways with pepperoni and pineapple, BBQ
chicken, and margarita style

Shrimp lettuce wraps with peanut sauce and pineapple salsa
Baked spaghetti
Chicken fajitas with red, orange, and green peppers, onions, and mango salsa
Pulled pork and coleslaw

Week 9
Short rib ragu street tacos with Asian slaw
Grilled steak with smashed potatoes and asparagus
Gnocchi with sundried tomatoes, gorgonzola, and pine nuts
Drunken noodles with shrimp and seasonal vegetables
Quiche with ham, broccoli, and cheddar cheese

Week 10
Shrimp pad Thai
Roasted chicken with potatoes, carrots, and celery
Cod fish tacos with pineapple salsa
Turkey pot pie
Chicken enchiladas

Week 11
Roasted chicken with baby red potatoes, carrots, and onions
Scallops with fresh basil and garlic butter over angel hair pasta
Drunken noodles with seasonal vegetables
Eggplant parmigiana
Roasted chicken noodle soup

Week 12
Coconut shrimp lettuce wraps with pineapple salsa and rice
Smash burgers with sweet potato fries and corn
Mushroom risotto with peas and asparagus
Chicken satay and orange chicken
Frittata with bacon, sausage, red peppers, onions, and cheddar cheese

Week 13
Spaghetti with meat sauce and garlic bread
Naan pizza three ways with pepperoni and pineapple, BBQ
chicken, and margarita style
Steak with sweet corn and fettuccini alfredo
Bang bang shrimp and cauliflower with basmati rice and Japanese
cucumber salad
Beef enchilada

Week 14
Huli-huli chicken with grilled pineapple
Loco moco
Beef fajitas with red, orange, and green peppers, onions, and
guacamole
Pulled pork with coleslaw
Tuna poke over rice

Week 15
Taco night with hard shells, ground beef, lettuce, tomato, and cheese
Lobster rolls with sweet corn on the cob and Cape Cod kettle chips
Vietnamese shaking beef over arugula
Spatchcock chicken with roasted potatoes and carrots
Portobello steak with parmesan and spinach stuffing

Week 16
Paella with shrimp, andouille sausage, and chicken thighs
BBQ ribs with sweet corn, cucumber onion salad, and mac and cheese
Pork chops with roasted Brussels sprouts and fingerling potatoes
Angel hair summer pasta with zucchini, asparagus, and peas
Eggplant parmesan over spaghetti noodles

Week 17
Vegetable stir-fry with drunken noodles
Smash burgers with sweet potato fries and special sauce
Salmon over coconut rice with corn on the cob
Pork adobo tacos with pineapple salsa

Meat lasagna with cream cheese, mozzarella, parmesan, and marinara served with garlic bread

Week 18
Hanger steak with roasted potato and stir-fried vegetables
Sea bass with pasta and asparagus
Pork tenderloin over creamy coconut and pineapple rice
Fried chicken and jerk chicken hot wings
Ground beef enchiladas

Week 19
Butter chicken over basmati rice
Caprese pasta with tomato, fresh mozzarella, basil, and garlic-infused olive oil
Cheeseburgers with grilled potato chips and mac and cheese
Halibut fish tacos with mango salsa
Naan pizza three ways with pepperoni and pineapple, BBQ chicken, and margarita style

Week 20
Glazed ham with honey glazed carrots and a side salad
Taco night with hard shells, ground beef, lettuce, tomato, and cheese
Sea bass with cauliflower rice and zucchini
Drunken noodles with chicken and seasonal vegetables
BBQ ribs with baked beans and cornbread

Week 21
Chicken lettuce wraps
Pasta carbonara and cacio e pepe
Scallops over asparagus risotto
Grilled steaks with baked potato and broccoli
Chicken parmesan

Week 22
BBQ chicken thighs with an avocado, corn, tomato, and basil salad
Salmon with Brussels sprouts and potatoes

Shrimp drunken noodles with broccoli and cauliflower
Steak fajitas with red, orange, and green peppers, onions, mango salsa, and guacamole
Pork chops with coleslaw and cucumber salad

Week 23
BBQ pork steaks with baked beans and potato salad
Baltimore-style crab cakes with cornbread and a strawberry, pear, and mozzarella salad
Salmon burgers with dill creme fraiche, grilled Brussels sprouts, and avocado salad
Korean short ribs over polenta
Chicken enchiladas

Week 24
Butternut squash ravioli with alfredo and roasted asparagus
Live Maine lobster with cornbread, mac and cheese, and corn on the cob
Taco night with hard shells, ground beef, lettuce, tomato, and cheese
Scallops over mascarpone polenta
Chili mac

Week 25
Roasted chicken with potatoes, carrots, and onions
Gnocchi with mushrooms, sun-dried tomatoes, and feta
Salmon with bok choy and cauliflower rice
Ramen noodle bowl with pork belly, hard-boiled eggs, radish, and bean sprouts
Live oyster night with champagne mignonette

Week 26
Hot wings with three sauces (jerk, buffalo, and lemon parmesan)
Moules Frites: Mussels and French fries
Bang bang shrimp and cauliflower with basmati rice and Japanese cucumber salad

Cod fish tacos with pineapple salsa and tortilla chips
Chicken pot pie

Week 27
Fettuccini with alfredo sauce and broccoli
Lobster rolls with kettle chips
Drunken noodles with chicken and seasonal vegetables
Steak with asparagus and au gratin potatoes
Minestrone soup

Week 28
Crab cakes over polenta
Steak fajitas with red, orange, and green peppers, onions, and
guacamole
Shrimp with fettuccine alfredo
BBQ ribs with cornbread and cucumber salad
Chicken tortilla soup

Week 29
Ramen noodle bowl with chicken thighs, hard-boiled eggs, radish,
and bean sprouts
Braised short ribs over polenta
Clams in white wine broth with arugula salad
Gnocchi with a gorgonzola cream sauce
Clam chowder

Week 30
Sesame chicken over rice with cauliflower and spinach
Salmon with roasted asparagus and roasted potatoes
Grilled burgers with hand-cut fries
THANKSGIVING DAY COOKING
Thanksgiving leftover turkey soup

Week 31
Taco night with hard shells, ground beef, lettuce, tomato, and cheese
Mushroom risotto with asparagus and truffles

Scallops over polenta with asparagus
Spaghetti and meatballs
Roasted chicken noodle soup

Week 32
Baked sea bass and zucchini over rice
Teriyaki chicken with cauliflower steak and Brussels sprouts
Halibut with leeks and mushrooms over arugula salad
Lemon risotto with asparagus
Chicken sausage tortellini soup

Week 33
Cheese ravioli with alfredo sauce and roasted asparagus
Sichuan pork with bok choy over cauliflower rice
Salmon over polenta with asparagus
Grilled ribeye with Swiss chard and mac and cheese
Chicken and orzo soup

Week 34
Crab cakes with polenta and a remoulade sauce
Taco night with hard shells, ground beef, lettuce, tomato, and cheese
Pasta tossed with sautéed vegetables and a creamy tomato sauce
Naan pizza three ways with pepperoni and pineapple, BBQ chicken, and margarita style
Live lobster and oysters for Christmas Eve

Week 35
Braised chuck roast street tacos with Asian slaw
Butternut squash ravioli with brown sage butter
Miso-glazed cod with roasted cauliflower over rice
Naan pizza three ways with pepperoni and pineapple, BBQ chicken, and margarita style
Lemon Greek chicken potato soup

Week 36
Mushroom risotto
Salmon with roasted potato and asparagus
Turkey lettuce wraps with dipping sauce
Caprese pasta and grilled steak
Chili mac

Week 37
Spaghetti and meatballs
Ramen noodle bowl with pork belly, hard-boiled eggs, radish, and bean sprouts
BBQ ribs with baked beans, potato salad, coleslaw, cornbread, and mac and cheese
Chicken Milanese with asparagus and arugula salad
Ground turkey and vegetable soup

Week 38
Roasted halibut with asparagus and a miso glaze
Taco night with hard shells, ground beef, lettuce, tomato, and cheese
Chicken stir-fry over basmati rice
T-bone steaks with roasted Brussels sprouts and baked potatoes
Minestrone soup

Week 39
Teriyaki chicken stir-fry with drunken noodles
Chicken parmesan
Scallops with mushroom and pea risotto
Pizza night
Broccoli cheddar soup

Week 40
Steak fajitas with red, orange, and green peppers, onions, and guacamole
Gnocchi with alfredo sauce
Halibut with sautéed vegetables over rice
Sichuan pork with broccoli over cauliflower rice

Meat lasagna with cream cheese, mozzarella, parmesan, and marinara served with garlic bread

Week 41
Shrimp tacos with mango and pineapple salsa
Pineapple fried rice with chicken
Grilled steak with a panzanella salad
Roasted chicken with potatoes, carrots, and onions
Pulled pork and coleslaw

Week 42
Salmon and asparagus with gnocchi
Caprese pasta with tomatoes, basil, fresh mozzarella, and garlic-infused olive oil
Chicken pot pie
Grilled burgers and hand-cut fries
Potato chowder

Week 43
Crab cakes and au gratin potatoes
Taco night with hard shells, ground beef, lettuce, tomato, and cheese
Broccoli beef over basmati rice
Chicken stir-fry with seasonal vegetables
Italian soup with Swiss chard

Week 44
Sea bass with Brussels sprouts and lemon beurre blanc
Butternut squash pasta with alfredo sauce
Arroz con pollo: Roasted chicken over rice
BBQ ribs with baked beans and coleslaw
Mulligatawny soup

Week 45
BBQ shrimp and grits
Chicken pad Thai and green curry chicken
Pork chops with sautéed broccoli and mushrooms

Salmon with roasted asparagus
Clam chowder

Week 46
Ground pork lettuce wraps with dipping sauce
Mussels in white wine with fettuccine alfredo
Chicken fajitas with red, orange, and green peppers, onions, and
guacamole
Corned beef and cabbage with roasted potatoes and Irish soda bread
Meat lasagna with cream cheese, mozzarella, parmesan, and mari-
nara served with garlic bread

Week 47
Broccoli beef over rice
Grilled steak with grilled potatoes and cauliflower steaks
Salmon with roasted asparagus
Summer pasta with zucchini, asparagus, and peas tossed with
garlic-infused olive oil
Chicken tortilla soup

Week: 48
Scallops with roasted Brussels sprouts
Taco night with hard shells, ground beef, lettuce, tomato, and cheese
Gnocchi carbonara
Salmon with sautéed green beans over basmati rice
Chili

Week 49
*OFF because one should always attend Opening Day at Busch Stadium
with the St. Louis Cardinals and pals Jen, Kim, Paula, Jill, and Audrey!
Since I was off for the week, I've added a menu of what I made a different week.*

Tri-tip with pickled red onions
Veal Marsala with mushrooms over rice
Sloppy Joe's with BBQ potato chips and bread & butter pickles

Cod fish tacos with mango salsa and guacamole
Chicken parmigiana over spaghetti noodles

Week 50
Shrimp and vegetable stir-fry over drunken noodles
Broccoli beef and mushrooms over rice
Angel hair caprese pasta with tomatoes, fresh mozzarella, basil, and garlic-infused olive oil
Mushroom risotto
Chicken orzo soup

Week 51
Crab cakes with polenta and arugula salad
Spaghetti night
Steak with grilled zucchini and asparagus
Rockfish tacos and mango salsa
Chicken parmesan over spaghetti noodles

Week 52
Grilled burgers with potato au gratin
Baked salmon with grilled vegetables
Scallop lettuce wraps with dipping sauce
Orange chicken and pineapple fried rice
Beef enchiladas

CHAPTER 10

ENTREES

"The day live animals start showing up, I'm out."

I AM BEGINNING THE ENTREE SECTION WITH DAY 1 and a signature dish of mine, Boeuf Bourguignon. From there, I have arranged the dishes alphabetically rather than by how they appear in the weekly menus for ease of finding the dish you want to cook tonight. I have kept that same idea of sorting alphabetically throughout each section.

As you prepare to cook each entree, keep in mind that I was cooking for a family of two adults and two kids, one of which couldn't fully eat all the food I was making. **Think about using a pound of protein with two to three of each of the vegetables and roughly one to two cups of starch as a rule of thumb as you go forward in this book.**

BOEUF BOURGUIGNON

MONDAY (DAY 1)

The first day. I was nervous, but I knew once I got in the kitchen and got moving, the food would calm me. Inspired by my favorite chef, Julia Child, I knew the first dish I had to make for the new family was a specialty of mine. If you follow the exact Julia recipe, it is quite daunting and time consuming, as evident by Julie Powell's memoir and subsequent movie, *Julie & Julia*. This was also a dish that Julia Child prepared on *The French Chef* on television in 1963. It's well worth it, trust me.

Beef, cubed
Bacon
Carrots
Onions
Tomato paste
Garlic
Flour
Red wine
Beef stock

NOTES

- Preheat oven to 450 degrees
- Cut bacon into strips and cook off until crispy, set aside
- Using store-bought stew meat, brown beef cubes in bacon grease; set aside and toss with flour to lightly coat
- Add carrots and sliced onions to the pot and sauté
- Add tomato paste and garlic, stirring to combine
- Put bacon and beef back in the pot
- In the oven, cook at 450 for 6-8 minutes to lightly brown the flour
- Reduce heat to 325 degrees
- Back on the stovetop, add red wine and beef stock to cover meat
- Cook covered for 2.5-3 hours in the 325-degree oven
- Serve over Amish noodles

AMISH NOODLE

Amish noodles are noodles made with egg yolks only to create a richer taste and golden color.

TIPS:
I use a Le Creuset pot, but any Dutch oven will do.

BAKED SPAGHETTI

Spaghetti noodles
Meat sauce or
marinara
Parmesan

NOTES

- Boil noodles
- Make your
  own sauce or
  use a jar of
  your favorite
  store-bought sauce
- Toss with noodles
- Add to a casserole dish
- Top with parmesan
- Bake at 350 degrees about 15-20 minutes until the cheese
  is melted

Modification:
Add some vegetables: zucchini, eggplant, peppers
Add some fresh mozzarella
Add a protein like chicken breast or thighs

We have a family dinner night once a week here in Frankfort. Mama
Burke's spaghetti is a favorite of mine, but every so often, it goes
into a casserole dish and gets baked with lots of mozzarella on top.
   Another fun twist is to turn chicken tenders into breaded
chicken and sneak them in with the spaghetti for a mashup of
baked spaghetti and chicken parmigiana.

BAKED ZITI

Ziti or mostaccioli
Ground beef
Marinara
Mozzarella
Basil
Parmesan
Salt
Pepper (or Chef Tara's
Spice Mix)

NOTES

This dish is inspired by my friend Harry D'Ercole, who owns Enrico's, an Italian restaurant in Frankfort, IL. Open since 1974, the Baked Mostaccioli, which is similar to this, is one of their most popular dishes.

As a personal chef, I am always looking for inspiration. Oftentimes, it's best to trust friends.

- Cook off pasta
- Add marinara or any tomato sauce to the browned ground beef
- Add seasonings
- Combine pasta with sauce and pour into a 9x11 baking dish
- Top with mozzarella and parmesan
- Bake at 375 for 15-20 minutes until the cheese is melted
- Top with fresh basil

Modification:
Make the day before
Cook at 375 for 30-35 minutes to heat through and melt cheese

BANG BANG CAULIFLOWER AND SHRIMP

Shrimp
Cauliflower
Mayonnaise
Sriracha
Thai chili sauce
Rice vinegar
Panko
Salt
Pepper
Paprika

NOTES

I looked at tons of different recipes to get this dish just right. Most called for an egg, flour, and panko breading. I tried something a little simpler.

- Mix the mayonnaise, sriracha, and Thai chili sauce together with a splash of rice vinegar to make your bang bang sauce
- Toss the cauliflower in some of the sauce to coat then add the panko
- Bake the cauliflower on a sheet pan at 425 degrees for about 15-18 minutes until the panko starts to brown

For the shrimp, I tossed mine with salt, pepper, and paprika and grilled them, about 3 minutes per side then tossed with the bang bang sauce.

You can also bread the shrimp with panko and bake it off as well, but grilled shrimp is just better sometimes.

BBQ CHICKEN

Chicken breast or
thighs
BBQ sauce of your
choice or make
your own
Salt
Pepper

NOTES

Preheat oven to 350
degrees or fire up the
grill.

Generously season your chicken with salt and pepper. While most people prefer chicken breast, I on the other hand am a huge chicken thigh fan. It is much more versatile to work with and has more flavor. Chicken thigh holds heat better and longer so as to not dry out.

You can cook these one of two ways: either on the grill, or on sheet pans in the oven at 350 degrees.

Cook the chicken for about 8-10 minutes on each side then begin adding the BBQ sauce, flipping and basting and continuing to cook until the internal temperature reaches 165 degrees.

BBQ RIBS

St. Louis style ribs
(or baby back if you
prefer)
BBQ dry rub
BBQ sauce of your
choice
Mustard (optional)

NOTES

- Generously apply dry rub to the ribs, using yellow or Dijon mustard as a binder for the spices by adding that to the ribs first
- Seal in aluminum foil
- Bake at 300 degrees for 2.5 hours
- Open foil and baste with BBQ sauce
- Cook for 5 minutes uncovered then baste a second time
- Cook for another 5 minutes then pull them out and let them rest about 5-10 minutes
- Cut the ribs apart and serve with baked beans and coleslaw

BBQ SHRIMP AND GRITS

Shrimp
Garlic
Worcestershire sauce
Heavy cream
Butter
Lemon juice
Hot sauce
Salt
Pepper
Paprika
Grits/polenta
Milk

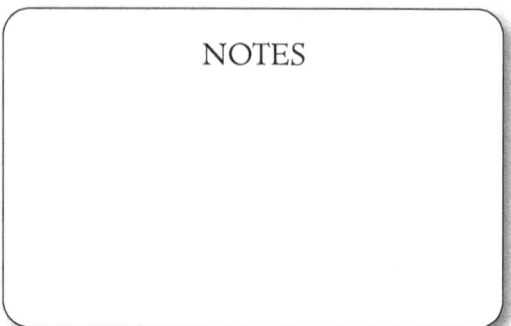

NOTES

- In a pot, add the grits and milk and cook, stirring frequently, according to the directions on the packaging
- Use peeled, deveined, tail-on shrimp and season with salt, pepper, and paprika
- In a wok or skillet, sauté garlic in butter
- Add Worcestershire sauce and heavy cream and whisk together
- Add shrimp and cook 3-4 minutes
- Finish with a squeeze of fresh lemon juice
- Plate the grits first then add the shrimp and finish with the sauce

BROCCOLI BEEF

Sirloin steak
Broccoli

Marinade:
Soy
Sesame oil
Cornstarch

Cooking sauce:
Rice wine vinegar
Oyster sauce
Cornstarch

NOTES

- Slice steak thin and marinade in the soy, sesame oil, and cornstarch for about 30 minutes or overnight
- Cut broccoli into florets
- In a hot wok, sauté beef and broccoli together
- Add cooking sauce

Serve over basmati, jasmine, or cauliflower rice

Modification:
Add red bell pepper for color
Add mushrooms or any other seasonal vegetables

BUTTER CHICKEN

Chicken thighs
Greek yogurt
Lemon juice
Turmeric
Garam marsala
Cumin
Butter
Yellow onion
Garlic
Ginger
Tomatoes
Chicken stock
Heavy cream
Tomato paste
Grapeseed oil
Salt

NOTES

- Marinate chicken thighs in yogurt, lemon juice, turmeric, garam masala, and cumin
- Melt butter in oil
- Add diced onions
- Add garlic and ginger
- Add diced tomatoes
- Add chicken and marinade
- Add chicken stock
- Bring everything to a boil
- Simmer uncovered for 30 minutes
- Stir in cream and tomato paste
- Simmer and let cook for 10-15 minutes until chicken reaches 165 degrees internally

Butter chicken is one of my favorite Indian dishes. When I lived in the Bay Area, I had an upstairs family of Indian descent, and whenever she made this dish, she would bring me dinner.

CACIO e PEPE

Pasta
Pecorino Romano
cheese
Pepper
Salt
Olive oil

NOTES

- Boil water with salt and add the noodles to cook
- You can use any noodle such as spaghetti or linguini
- In a bowl, add the cheese and the pepper, mixing in a bit of pasta water to create a paste
- Once the pasta is cooked to al dente, add it to the bowl with the cheese and the pepper paste, stirring to coat the pasta
- Use olive oil to thin it out as needed
- Finish the dish by plating and adding more cheese and pepper

Another simple yet delicious pasta dish.

CAPRESE PASTA

Fettuccine, linguine, or
pappardelle
Tomato, whole or
cherry tomatoes
Mozzarella
Basil
Garlic
Olive oil
Salt

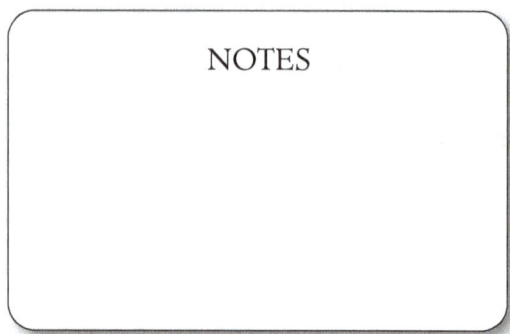

NOTES

- Infuse oil with sliced garlic cloves the day before if time allows
- Using a big white bowl, add the chunked tomato, mozzarella, and torn basil into the bowl
- You can also just halve cherry tomatoes
- Cook pasta in salted pasta water
- Don't strain the pasta, instead, use a hand strainer and lift the hot pasta and some water into your bowl as the pasta water will help everything bind together
- Top with shredded parmesan and garlic-infused oil

Modification:

If you can't infuse the garlic overnight, simply roast off some cloves in oil at 375 degrees for about 30-40 minutes.

Francesca's, our local restaurant in town and my favorite, is often a great source of inspiration for all things Italian. This dish is a popular one amongst my friends, so I tried to replicate it with a few tweaks.

CARBONARA

Pasta
Eggs
Guanciale (cured pork,
diced pancetta, or
bacon)
Pecorino Romano
cheese
Pepper
Salt

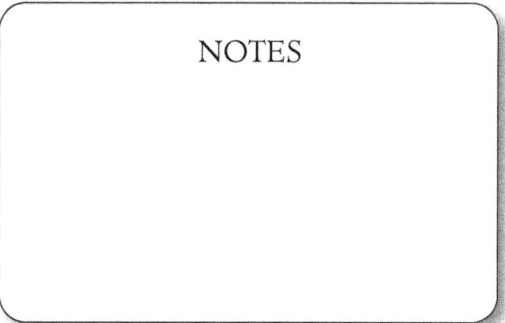

NOTES

- Boil water with salt and add the noodles to cook
- You can use any noodle such as spaghetti or linguini
- In a bowl, add a couple of eggs and a couple of egg yolks and mix that together with the cheeses
- Season this with salt and a good amount of black pepper
- In a skillet, sauté the pork until it gets crispy and set aside
- Once the pasta boils to al dente, add it to the skillet with the egg mixture
- Stir to create a creamy consistency
- Add the pork back in and finishing the dish with more pepper and some grated cheese

Simple yet delicious.

CHEF TARA'S TRI-TIP WITH PICKLED RED ONIONS

Tri-tip
Balsamic vinegar
Chef Tara's Spice Mix
Olive oil
Pickled red onions

NOTES

- Marinate tri-tip overnight in a gallon-size Ziploc bag with the balsamic, seasonings, and olive oil
- Over a hot grill, sear the tri-tip (there will be flames) for 5 minutes each side
- Lower the grill temperature to about medium-high heat and continue cooking for 13-15 minutes, flipping halfway through, until the center is still a bit rare
- Pull the tri-tip when the internal temperature reads about 130-135, then let it rest for 10 minutes
- Slice and serve with pickled red onions
- Make sliders or serve as an entrée

CHICKEN CURRY

Chicken thighs
Thai basil
Bamboo shoots
Red bell pepper
Green curry paste
Coconut milk
Fish sauce
Sugar
Chicken stock

NOTES

- In a pot, reduce coconut milk until it starts to thicken
- Toss chicken with the curry paste and add to the coconut milk
- Add chicken stock
- Simmer for 10-15 minutes
- Add lime zest, fish sauce, sugar, bamboo shoots, and red bell peppers
- Make sure the internal temp of the chicken is 165 degrees

This is a favorite of the father of the house, so it's a treat to make it for him. Don't let the word "Curry" intimidate you. We all know that Steph Curry from the Golden State Warriors is one of the best basketball players to play the game, and he can be intimidating on the court. But THIS curry couldn't be easier and it's so good. You could literally put everything in a pot at once and let it cook like a soup.

I royally fucked up the curry one night simply because I didn't look at what I was putting in the pot. I had ordered coconut milk, when instead, I had received a coconut plant-based milk, like an almond milk that one might put into their coffee. So instead of the hearty, meaty coconut milk in the can that needs to cook down to thicken, I was using a watery broth. It didn't absorb the curry paste as it should, so it was so watery and spicy it was completely inedible.

The lesson here is, always know what you are putting in your dish. Which also goes back to always tasting throughout the cooking process. Add and taste, add and taste.

CHICKEN MILANESE

Chicken breast
Flour
Egg
Panko
Salt
Pepper (or Chef Tara's
Spice Mix)
Grated parmesan
Olive oil

NOTES

- Pound the chicken breast nice and thin by cutting it in half first
- Use a meat mallet to pound the two sides into nice thin filets (I put my chicken in a plastic zip lock bag before I pound it out as to not splatter the chicken "juice" around the kitchen and eliminate unnecessary contamination)
- Season the chicken, the flour, and the panko with salt and pepper (or Chef Tara's Spice Mix)
- Dredge the chicken using the standard breading procedure: first the flour, then egg, then finally the panko
- Add the chicken to a sauté pan with hot oil and cook about 3 minutes each side until golden brown
- Make sure the internal temp is 165 degrees before serving
- Serve over an arugula parmesan salad with a lemon vinaigrette

STANDARD BREADING PROCEDURE

The Standard Breading Procedure has three steps:

1. **Dredge in flour**
2. **Moisten in the egg wash, which is simply a beaten egg (you can add a dash of milk but it's not necessary)**
3. **Coat in breadcrumbs or my favorite, Panko**

CHICKEN or EGGPLANT PARMIGIANA

Chicken breast filets or
eggplant
Flour
Egg
Panko
Olive oil
Marinara
Mozzarella
Parmesan
Salt
Pepper (Or Chef Tara's Spice Mix)

NOTES

I usually try and make this the day before as it's a popular weekend dish the family can just heat up. If you are serving this immediately:

- Season and bread chicken breast using the standard breading procedure with flour, egg, then panko
- Bake chicken at 350 degrees for about 25-30 minutes
- Top with marinara, mozzarella, and parmesan and put back in the oven another 15 minutes or so until the cheese is melty and internal temp reaches 165 degrees

Modification:

Make it vegetarian and use eggplant instead. Simply slice the eggplant into about half-inch rounds and apply salt and let it sit for about 10 minutes to pull excess water out. Once dried, follow the steps above by breading the eggplant and baking at 350 degrees for about 25-30 minutes. Then add the marinara, mozzarella, and parmesan and bake again for another 15 minutes or so until the cheese is melty.

I like to use cooked pasta (spaghetti or penne) as a base layer to set the chicken on.

CHICKEN SATAY

Chicken thighs
Coconut milk
Yellow curry
Brown sugar
Turmeric
Fish sauce
Soy sauce
Peanut sauce for
dipping

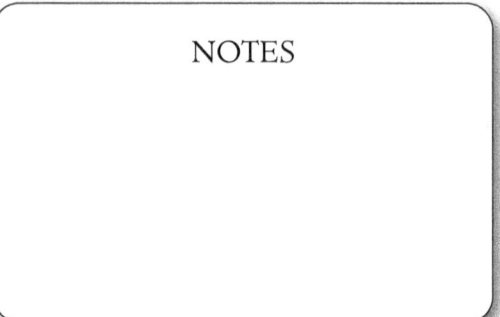

NOTES

- Make the marinade
- Dice chicken and marinate overnight if possible
- Skewer the chicken, then use a grill pan to cook the chicken, turning frequently until the internal temp reaches 165 degrees

COCONUT SHRIMP

Jumbo shrimp
Flour
Egg
Panko
Unsweetened shredded
coconut
Salt
Pepper
Orange marmalade
Thai chili sauce
Soy sauce

NOTES

When purchasing the shrimp, use the jumbo size, peeled, deveined, and tail on.

- Mix panko with coconut, salt, and pepper
- Dredge shrimp in flour, egg, and panko using the standard breading procedure
- Fry the shrimp in a skillet with oil about 1-1.5 minutes per side until golden brown
- Make the dipping sauce from the marmalade, Thai chili sauce, and soy sauce
- Serve over rice with a side of stir-fried vegetables

COD FISH TACOS

Cod filet
Olive oil
Salt
Pepper
Butter lettuce or soft
taco tortillas
Radicchio
Cabbage
Scallions

NOTES

- Season fish on both sides
- Bake at 400 degrees for 8-10 minutes until internal temperature reaches 125 degrees and the fish is flaky
- Make an Asian slaw with the radicchio, cabbage, and scallions and toss with an Asian vinaigrette
- Fill either lettuce cups or the tortillas with cod and Asian slaw
- Add guacamole and hot sauce if your palate calls for it

CORNED BEEF AND CABBAGE

Corned beef
Red baby potatoes
Green cabbage
Salt
Pepper
Brine

NOTES

- Quarter cabbage
- Halve the potatoes
- Slow braise the corned beef at 300 degrees for 4.5 hours in Guinness and water covering three-quarters of the beef
- Add potatoes and cabbage leaves the last 45 minutes of cooking time

We order American wagyu corned beef brisket every year from Snake River Farms in Idaho. It comes already brined, so it's ready to go into the oven.

For a trusted brine, use Alton Brown's recipe on Food Network. com. He combines salt, sugar, cinnamon stick, mustard seeds, peppercorns, cloves, allspice, juniper berries, bay leaves, and ginger with about 6-8 quarts of water. Bring that to a boil and let it cool completely.

Add the brisket and the brine to a Ziploc bag and refrigerate for 10 days.

CRAB CAKES

Lump crab meat
Panko or saltines
Eggs
Worcestershire
Mayo
Chives
Dijon
Old Bay seasoning
Lemon juice
Parsley
Dill
Celery
Scallions
Unsalted butter

NOTES

- Mix the crab with all the ingredients, minus the butter. Save that for the pan to fry the cakes in
- Brush both sides of the crab cake with melted butter
- Fry 3 minutes then flip
- Continue cooking for another 2 minutes until nicely browned on both sides
- You can also bake the crab cakes on a sheet pan lined with parchment paper at 450 degrees for 12-14 minutes
- Serve with tartar sauce or remoulade sauce

Make them small for a crab cake appetizer or large for an entree.

DAD'S CHILI

Onion
Hamburger meat
Tomato juice
Tomato soup
Tomato paste
Tomato sauce
Kidney beans
Chili powder
Cayenne
Salt
Pepper
Sugar

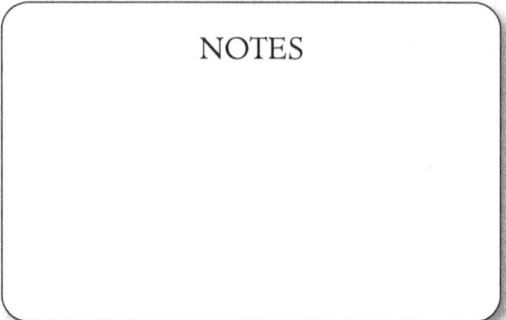

NOTES

This is the only recipe you will see with measurements in this book because the photo of Dad's chicken scratch of a recipe is the best.

When we were kids, there was nothing more we looked forward to than Dad's chili. He would start it in the morning and by mid-day, the aroma from that magical pot of goodness was enough to make our stomach grumble.

Over the course of twenty or so years, he would futz with the actual measurements until he felt like he had it nailed.

To this day, no other chili stacks up for me, and you can only serve it with Saltine crackers. Do not come at me with oyster crackers, cheese, or onions.

But the family I cook for loves all those things, plus avocado, so that is what they get!

- Start by browning the ground beef and the onions
- Then start opening all the cans and jars of all things tomato and adding to the pot
- Finally add the beans and all the seasonings and continue to stir until it starts to come to a boil, then lower the temperature and let it simmer all day, stirring occasionally to not burn the bottom.

Dad has since switched to using a crock pot for ease of use so he can just put all the things in first thing in the morning and let it slow cook all day.

Modification:
Cook off pasta noodles for a good chili mac.

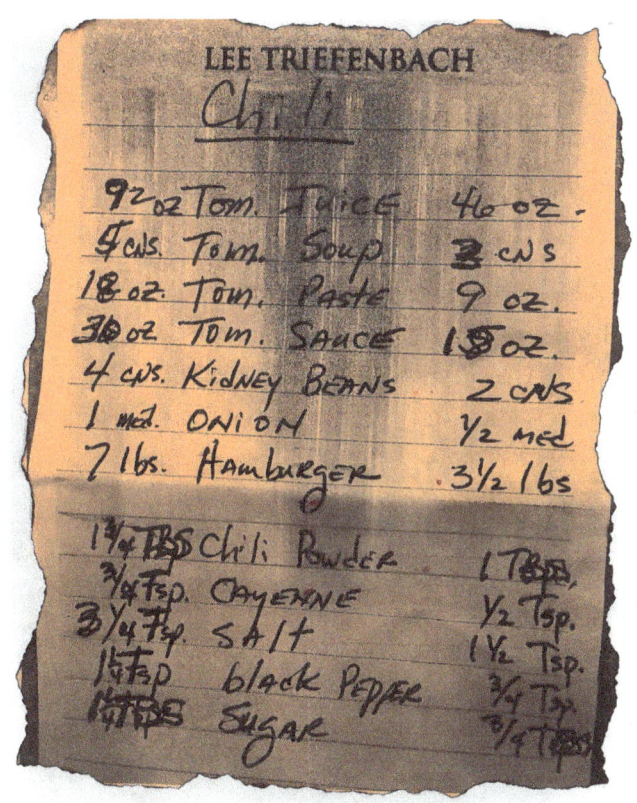

DRUNKEN NOODLES (Pad Kee Mao)

Wide rice noodles
Soy sauce
Fish sauce
Oyster sauce
Garlic
Thai basil (regular basil
works fine)
Sugar
Water
Chicken or shrimp
Steak or ground pork

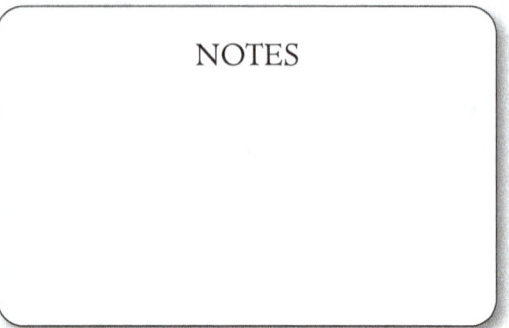

NOTES

- Soak the noodles for about 30-45 minutes
- Make the sauce from the soy, fish, and oyster sauces with garlic, sugar, and water
- Prep your protein by either dicing the chicken, slicing the steak, or cleaning the shrimp making sure it is peeled, deveined, with the tail off
- Sauté garlic and scallion
- Add protein
- Add noodles, strained
- Add sauce
- Sauté over high heat until the noodles absorb the sauce and get browned

Modification:
Add red bell pepper for color
Add any vegetable you
would like

The meal is often consumed
after a night of drinking in

Thailand, thus the name. If I saw this at a food stall at 1:00 a.m., I would want to eat all of it. But who am I kidding, I am in PJ's by about 7:15 p.m.

"As with many traditional dishes, there are several stories about where the name 'drunken noodles' came from. More than one of them is related to how spicy these noodles are. One explanation is that because the dish is so spicy, you would have to drink a lot to handle the spice. Another is that the extreme spice of the noodles is the only thing strong enough for inebriated people to taste. (giantofsiam.com).

ENCHILADAS (CHICKEN OR BEEF)

Soft taco tortillas
Rotisserie or roasted
chicken or ground beef
with taco seasoning
Shredded cheddar
cheese
Enchilada sauce

NOTES

- Toss chicken or beef with part of the enchilada sauce to coat
- You can make your own enchilada sauce or use a pre-made jar
- Using soft taco size tortillas, add chicken or beef mix and some of the cheddar or Mexican cheese blend
- Roll up the tortilla like a cigar and add to a glass baking dish (1/2 pan), continuing with the five other tortillas until the dish is full
- Cover with enchilada sauce and top with cheese
- Bake at 375 for about 30-35 minutes until heated through

This will make six enchiladas in total.

FAJITAS

Steak or chicken
Red pepper
Orange pepper
Yellow pepper
Yellow onion
Corn or flour tortillas
Salt
Paprika
Onion powder
Garlic powder
Cayenne
Oregano

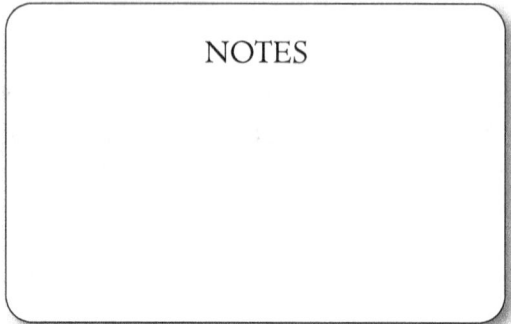

NOTES

- Slice raw steak into strips (this is easier to do if partially frozen)
- Julienne peppers and onions, meaning to cut them into strips
- Toss all proteins and vegetables with the seasonings
- Sauté in a hot wok with some grapeseed oil
- Serve with guacamole and salsa

Modification:
Grill the steak then slice into strips
Grill the onion and peppers, partially whole, then cut into strips.

FETTUCCINE ALFREDO

Fettuccini noodles
Heavy cream
Garlic
Parmesan
Salt
Pepper (or Chef Tara's
Spice Mix)

NOTES

- In a pot, add heavy cream, garlic, and parmesan cheese and bring to a boil
- Let simmer about 5-6 minutes being careful not to burn
- Boil pasta and toss with the alfredo

Modification:
Add shrimp; peeled, deveined, tail off
Add chicken

FISH FRY FRIDAY

Cod filets
Salt
Pepper
Cornmeal mix

NOTES

Fried cod has a spe-
cial place in my heart
because of Fish Fry
Friday. Ever since I was
a kid, every Friday we
would go to the VFW or the Catholic Charities spots down the
country road from our house to have fish. Ott's Tavern in Millstadt,
IL, was also a regular fish joint we would frequent.

Last summer, I met Terry, the owner of Ott's Tavern, and I
picked his brain. We talked about all things fish and how the heck
he made it so good. I told him I wanted to try and replicate it for
the family I cook for. So, he took me into the kitchen and showed
me how the magic happens.

Using the cod we get from Alaska, one Friday night I tried to
replicate it. It turned out to be about 92.6 percent accurate from
the original recipe. I still need to tweak it a bit, so maybe this summer I will get it just right. But I don't know if anyone can duplicate
what Terry does at Ott's Tavern, nor should they because it's perfect
in my opinion.

Grandma Walton used to make a beer batter for all the crappie
we used to catch at Lake Shelbyville in central Illinois. We grew up
fishing there with Grandpa and the Ding-A-Lings (my grandma
and her sisters), and we would pull in fresh crappie like it was our
job. I learned how to filet a fish at a very young age, which came
in handy in culinary school. Her beer batter recipe was just cornmeal, salt, pepper, and beer. I have burnt my tongue many times
on fried crappie because we couldn't wait to eat it once it came
out of the fryer.

FRIED CHICKEN AND HOT WINGS

Chicken drumsticks
Chicken wings
Buttermilk
Flour
Salt
Pepper
Oil

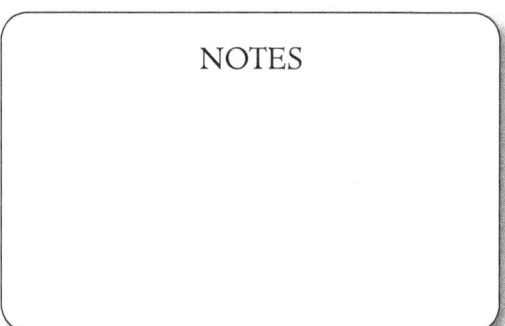

NOTES

The fried chicken is pretty straight forward, I hope. Let the chicken soak in the buttermilk for 30 minutes or more then toss with the flour, salt, and pepper mixture. Then, you can do it one of two ways: frying in hot oil for 30-40 minutes or simply baking them in the oven at 350 degrees for 30 minutes, flipping and cooking for 30 minutes more until the internal temperature reaches 165 degrees.

Hot wings are a different story. I don't like too much of a breading on hot wings. My Seester and I are hot wing connoisseurs and have had them just about everywhere. I have found a grilled hot wing to be delightful and I am an "all flats" kind of girl with buffalo sauce. At Buffalo Wild Wings, try the mild sauce with the salt and vinegar dry rub. You're welcome.

For these hot wings, I did not bread them, instead I baked them off until crispy. Toss the wings with olive oil, salt, and pepper and put on a baking rack, cooking for about 30 minutes at 450 degrees. Make sure the internal temperature is 165 degrees then toss with Buffalo sauce, Caribbean jerk sauce, and lemon parmesan sauce.

FRITTATA AND QUICHE

Yukon gold potatoes
Butter
Meat: bacon, sau-
sage, ham
Vegetable: peppers,
broccoli, mushrooms
or anything seasonal of
your choosing
Eggs
Milk
Shredded cheddar cheese

NOTES

- Combine about eight eggs with some milk and set aside
- Brown diced potatoes in a cast-iron skillet with butter
- Add meats and vegetables, any combination you choose
- Pour in the egg and milk mixture
- Finish with shredded cheddar cheese
- Bake at 350 degrees for 50 minutes to an hour

**Make it a quiche by adding it to a pie crust instead of using the cast-iron skillet. Brown the potatoes, meats, and vegetables then add to the pie crust and top with the egg mixture. Bake according to the pie crust recipe on the package.

A frittata or quiche is perfect for an overnight sleepover breakfast. My Frannie Pack and I go to Long Beach, IN, every summer for four days to rest, relax, recharge, and act like our eighteen-year-old college selves for a lot of laughter. The frittata for the morning after is perfect to soak up the alcohol from the night before and provide protein for the new day at the beach.

GLAZED HAM

Fresh ham butt
or shank
Salt
Pepper
Molasses
Balsamic vinegar
Cinnamon
Toasted pecans
Candied ginger

NOTES

- Score the ham by cutting nice big slits into the outer layer and generously season with salt and pepper
- Cook ham in a 450-degree oven for about 20 minutes
- While the ham is cooking, make the glaze of molasses, balsamic vinegar, and cinnamon
- Baste the ham with the glaze
- Turn the oven down to 300 degrees and cook for 2.5 to 3 hours, basting every half to one hour until the internal temperature reaches 145 degrees
- Toast pecans and combine with candied ginger in a food processor to create a crumbly garnish for the ham

GNOCCHI, RAVIOLI, AND TORTELLINI

- Bring a large pot of water to boil with salt and some olive oil
- Add the pasta of your choice and cook until they are floating on the top, about 3-4 minutes
- Toss with your sauce and serve with a nice side salad

NOTES

The girls love these three dishes with the simple creamy alfredo

Full disclosure, I had an EPIC GNOCCHI FAIL. I tried to make homemade gnocchi from leftover mashed potatoes after Thanksgiving. Typically, adding the leftover to flour and an egg should result in cute little potato pillows, right? Not so much and the reason being was, I couldn't use an egg due to the FPIES of the littlest little. I tried to get creative and find a substitute for the egg, but it turned into a giant mess. Just buy a good brand you trust and call it a day. Get creative with your sauces and sides instead.

(I did try again and successfully made gnocchi with the egg, but not for the three-year-old.)

Modification:

Add any cheese to the alfredo such as blue cheese or gorgonzola

Butternut squash ravioli in week 24 is fantastic with a brown butter sage sauce

In week 9, I made a gorgonzola cream sauce with sun-dried tomatoes and pine nuts

If using mushroom ravioli, use sliced mushrooms in the sauce for more umami.

HALIBUT WITH LEEK AND MUSHROOMS

Halibut
Flour
Leeks
Shitake mushrooms
White wine
Butter
Olive oil
Parsley

NOTES

- Season halibut
  with salt and pepper and dust with flour
- Sauté fish in an ovenproof skillet searing on each side about 2-3 minutes until a light brown crust forms
- Put the fish and the skillet into a 400-degree oven for about 3-5 minutes, until the internal temperature is 125 degrees
- Pull the fish and let it rest
- In that same sauté pan, cook leeks and mushrooms in oil and season with salt
- Add white wine then finish with butter so the sauce thickens a bit
- Plate the halibut over a parmesan arugula salad and finish with the mushroom leek sauce

I got this idea from a chef in Alaska. Our monthly shipment of fresh seafood often came with ideas for the items we received. This dish was simple and delicious for a beautiful presentation.

HULI-HULI CHICKEN

Chicken thighs
Fresh pineapple slices
Olive oil
Scallions

Marinade:
Brown sugar
Ketchup
Canned pineapple juice
Soy sauce
Worcestershire sauce
Apple cider vinegar
Ginger
Paprika
Pepper

NOTES

- Make the marinade using half of it for the chicken to soak in overnight (or 4-6 hours), and the other half to baste the chicken while cooking
- Grill chicken for about 5-6 minutes, then flip and baste
- Cook for about 4-5 minutes, then flip and baste again
- Continue this until the chicken reaches an internal temperature of 165 degrees, about 15-18 minutes
- Grill pineapple slices until you see nice grill marks, about 4 minutes per side
- Plate the pineapple slices down first then top with the chicken thigh and garnish with the scallions

Pro tip: Put the marinade in a pot, bring it to a boil, then let it simmer until plating. Use it to drizzle over the finished dish. This will kill the contamination from the raw protein and gives you a nice, hot, finishing sauce.

KOREAN SHORT RIB TACOS

Short ribs flanken
cut (ask your favorite
butcher)
Onion
Garlic
Ginger
Soy sauce
Brown sugar
Rice vinegar
Gochujang
Sesame oil
Pear or apple
Kiwi
Orange juice
Sprite
Corn or flour tortillas, street taco size
Scallions
Sesame seeds
Tortillas
Asian slaw

- Puree the ingredients, minus the ribs, in a blender to make the marinade, saving just a little for a sauce
- Sear the ribs in a cast-iron pot until browned on all sides then pour the marinade over the ribs
- Slow braise at 275 degrees for 3-4 hours
- Make an Asian slaw
- Top tortillas with meat and slaw and garnish with scallions and sesame seeds

Modification:

Add your favorite salsa or go simple with diced onions and cilantro.

Grill the ribs instead of braising and pull the meat off the bones.

Roy Choi put Kogi Korean BBQ on the map in LA back in 2008. When I was working at Reed College in Portland, I was the global chef for one year, which meant that I was tasked with cooking a different country's cuisine each week, a different dish every day. During Korea week, I instantly thought of this recipe as it had exploded in pop culture at the time.

LASAGNA

Tomato sauce
Tomato paste
Ground beef
Cream cheese
Mozzarella
Ricotta (I don't use
ricotta but please do if
you love it)
Parmesan
No-bake lasagna
noodles
Oregano
Salt
Pepper (or Chef Tara's Spice Mix)

NOTES

- Brown ground beef and add marinara
- Mix all cheeses together in a bowl and season with oregano
- Layer all ingredients starting with the sauce, noodles, then cheese, repeating three times and finishing with shredded mozzarella
- Bake at 375 degrees for 50-55 minutes covered, the last 5 minutes uncovered

My favorite lasagna is at Beppe & Gianni's in Eugene, OR. They make fresh handmade pasta that gets layered with their tomato sauce and béchamel, fresh beef, Italian sausage, and topped with mozzarella and parmesan. To say it's a little bit of heaven is an understatement. I used to travel for work up to Eugene, and I couldn't go back to San Francisco without having this meal.

If you want to get creative, make a bechamel sauce (see Sauces) and add Italian sausage to the mix.

LETTUCE WRAPS

Ground chicken
Bibb or butter lettuce
Water chestnuts
Mushrooms
Scallion

NOTES

Cooking Sauce:
Soy
Mirin
Oyster
Rice vinegar

Dipping Sauce:
Sugar
Soy
Rice vinegar
Chili oil
Scallions
Hot Chinese mustard
Sriracha

- Brown ground chicken
- Add water chestnuts and mushrooms
- Add sauce and let simmer about 10 minutes
- Fill lettuce cup with chicken mixture
- Garnish with scallions and dip away

Everyone loves PF Chang's chicken lettuce wraps. I modeled this dish after an amazing experience eating it.

Modification:
I like to make an Asian slaw of cabbage and carrots tossed with a vinaigrette of rice vinegar, grapeseed oil, Lahtt sauce, and honey.

Other proteins to use:
Ground turkey
Ground pork
Shrimp, peeled, deveined, tail off; seasoned with paprika, salt, and pepper

LOBSTER ROLL

Lump lobster meat, fully cooked
Or
2-3 live lobsters fully cooked
Celery
Mayo
Lemon juice
Salt
Unsalted butter
Brioche top-split hot dog buns

NOTES

If you can find lump lobster meat, that works perfectly, otherwise buy tails, boil about 5 minutes, then pull out the meat.

- In a bowl mix lobster meat with mayo, celery, lemon juice, and salt
- Brush sides of buns with butter then using a griddle pan, toast the bread
- Fill with lobster meat

You must serve this with good Cape Cod potato chips on the side!

My first lobster roll was out in Falmouth, MA, on the cape with my friend Maggie's family. I was spoiled that weekend with preparations of all things lobster made to perfection.

When I finally decided to menu this for the family, as requested, I immediately texted Maggie. I hope I made her family proud.

Martha Stewart has a simple, yet delicious recipe if you choose to look that up. I use celery very finely diced in mine for just a bit of crunch.

LOCO MOCO

Ground beef
Worcestershire sauce
Garlic powder
Salt
Pepper (or Chef Tara's
Spice Mix)
Beef stock
Soy sauce
Ketchup
Cornstarch
Butter
Mushrooms
Yellow onion
White rice
Eggs
Scallions

NOTES

- Make burger patties with the Worcestershire and seasonings
- Cook off burgers either on the grill or in a skillet and set aside
- In a bowl, make a gravy mix with beef stock, soy sauce, Worcestershire, ketchup, and cornstarch
- Melt butter in a skillet and fry mushrooms and onions
- Add gravy mix to this and stir to combine and thicken
- Fry egg sunny-side up or how you prefer to eat your fried egg
- Make white rice using the directions on the packet
- Usually 2 cups water to 1 cup white rice

To assemble the Loco Moco:

- On a plate add a scoop of white rice using an ice cream scooper
- Place the hamburger patty on top of the rice

- Pour the gravy over "all the things"
- Place the fried egg on top of this glorious pile of food and garnish with scallions

Grab a spoon, a ladle, a knife and fork, whatever you want to use to shovel this deliciousness into your face.

Loco = Crazy
Moco = Burger

"First reports of loco moco came from Hilo, HI, in 1949 when young, broke surfers needed something cheap, big, and loaded with carbs. A request for rice, beef, and gravy was given to Nancy Inouney of the Lincoln Grill. They named it after their friend George Okimoto, whose nickname was 'crazy.' George Takahashi, a student at Hilo High School, was studying Spanish and inserted 'loco' into this. The word 'moco' was added because it rhymed." (cafe100.com)

NAAN PIZZA

Naan bread
Pizza sauce
Butter
Garlic
Chef Tara's Spice Mix

NOTES

Use whatever pizza toppings you like. Our favorites at the house are pepperoni and pineapple, BBQ chicken with red onions, and a caprese with just fresh mozzarella, basil, and tomatoes.

- Brush the naan with melted butter, garlic, and Chef Tara's Spice Mix
- Bake in the oven at 425 degrees for 3 minutes
- Add pizza sauce and toppings
- Bake again about 10-12 minutes until the cheese starts to melt

Naan is a flatbread commonly found in Asian and Indian cuisines consisting of flour, salt, yeast, and water.

Modification:
Grill the naan first then add the toppings and continue to grill until the cheese melts.

ORANGE CHICKEN

Chicken breast
and thigh
Orange juice
Sugar
Rice vinegar
Soy sauce
Cornstarch
Water

NOTES

For my orange chicken,
I did it a little different than most recipes as I don't like a lot of breading. I simply diced the chicken and soaked it in soy sauce for about a half hour while I was prepping everything else I needed to do for that meal. Then, I tossed the chicken with panko and cooked it in the wok with hot olive oil, letting it fry to a nice brown color on all sides.

Once cooked to an internal temperature of 165 degrees, I then tossed it in the orange sauce.

For the orange sauce, I added orange juice, sugar, rice vinegar, and soy sauce to a pot and brought it to a boil then let it simmer. Make a "slurry" out of cornstarch and water and slowly add this to the pot, whisking as you pour, to create a thicker, saucier consistency.

OYSTERS, CLAMS, AND MUSSELS

We order our shellfish from Hog Island Oyster Co. out in Tomales Bay, CA. If you ever get a chance to head west, go sit at the picnic tables on the bay and order some oysters on the half shell with their Hog Wash and a cold Pinot Grigio or a beer and you will be the happiest person in that moment.

Oysters are easy. Just shuck 'em, add some mignonette, and slurp 'em down.

Or you can bake them with a recipe that the Buckeye Roadhouse in Marin, CA, used to serve.

Mayo
Spinach
Garlic
Lemon juice
Parmesan

NOTES

- Sauté the spinach in oil then strain out all the liquid
- Add the spinach to the mayo, minced garlic, lemon juice, and parmesan
- Add a nice spoonful to each shucked oyster and bake at 425 degrees for about 3 minutes

Clams and Mussels:

Clams
Mussels
Butter
White wine
Garlic
Chicken stock
Salt

NOTES

Clean them well under running water. Pull the "beard" off the mussels.

No, the "beard" is not the character Coach Beard from *Ted Lasso*. The beard on the mussels are byssal threads that mussels use to attach themselves to rocks. They are on the side of the mussel and are easy to remove by just pulling downward and out.

- Add some butter, white wine, and garlic to a Dutch oven and bring to a boil
- Add a little chicken stock and a bit of salt
- Add the shellfish to the pot and put the lid on for about 4-5 minutes until they open
- Serve with a crusty bread

PAD THAI

Grapeseed oil
Minced garlic
Chicken diced
Eggs
Pad Thai noodles
(soaked for 30-40
minutes)
Raw shrimp, peeled,
deveined, tail on
Pad Thai sauce
Bean sprouts
Crushed peanuts
Scallions

Pad Thai sauce:
Brown sugar
Fish sauce
Tamarind
Oyster sauce
Soy sauce

Chicken and shrimp pad Thai: My arch nemesis.

When I was in culinary school, the Bobby Flay of Thailand came to visit for a week: Chef DeNang. For that whole week, we had to practice making and perfecting pad Thai.

Phillip and I were a team, and on that Friday, we had a team competition and we were judged on

> NOTES

technical skills, flavor, and presentation. The winning team won a trip to Thailand.

After much sweat and constant stirring, we ended up losing by one point. We couldn't believe it, and I vowed never to eat or cook pad Thai ever again. Fortunately, I had to break my vow, but it was well worth it as it is a family favorite.

The key to pad Thai is your mise en place: putting things in order.

- Gather all your ingredients and have them ready to fire
- Soak pad Thai noodles in water for about 30-45 minutes before cooking
- In a wok: add grapeseed oil
- Add some minced garlic
- Add chicken breast or thighs diced and cook for about 1-2 minutes
- Push to side of wok
- Add a couple of eggs to the middle of oil and sauté
- Combine with ingredients in the pan
- Add noodles and cook 2-3 minutes
- Add shrimp and continue cooking
- Add sauce
- Incorporate half of the bean sprouts, peanuts, and scallions
- Cook until the shrimp are done, about 2-3 minutes
- Garnish with the rest of the bean sprouts, peanuts, scallions, and lime juice

PAELLA

Chicken thighs,
bone-in, skin on
Andouille sausage
Shrimp
Rice
Onion
Garlic
Red bell pepper
Roma tomatoes
Paprika
Saffron threads
Chicken stock
Frozen peas
Salt
Pepper
Bay leaf
Parsley
Olive oil

I am thankful to have a real paella pan, but any skillet or cast-iron skillet will work, just make sure it's big enough to hold 1-2 cups of rice and about 4-6 cups of broth.

- Add olive oil to the pan and sear off the chicken to brown the skin then set aside
- Do the same with the sliced andouille sausage, browning on both sides and setting aside
- Sauté the diced onion, garlic, and bell pepper until garlic is just browned and the onion is translucent
- Add the diced tomatoes, saffron, bay leaf, salt, and pepper and stir together, cooking another 3 minutes or so
- Add a bit of white wine to help deglaze the pan, cooking another 5 minutes
- Taste at this point and add more salt if needed

- Add about 1 cup of rice to the pan and stir to combine
- Add about 4 cups of chicken stock to cover rice
- Put the chicken thighs and sausage back in, and cook over high heat about 5 minutes
- Reduce the heat to low and cook about 15-20 minutes
- Season your shrimp and add it to the pan
- Keep simmering about another 10 minutes until the rice is al dente and has absorbed most of the liquid
- When the bottom of the dish is nice and golden brown and the shrimp and chicken are fully cooked to temp, the dish is ready
- Garnish with fresh parsley and serve in the skillet

You want the "Socarrat" at the bottom of the pan, which is the well-done crispy crunchy layer of rice underneath all the yummy goodness. After the broth cooks out, the rice starts to fry underneath. This is the best part, so don't think you are burning the dish.

PINEAPPLE FRIED RICE

Carrots
Peas
Pineapple
Arborio rice
Soy sauce

NOTES

- Cook off rice the day before if possible
- If not, cook the rice and let it sit in the refrigerator for at least 30 minutes to an hour
- In a wok, sauté the carrots and pineapple that have been diced
- Add the rice and soy sauce and continue to sauté
- Finish with the peas and serve with any protein of your choice and seasonal vegetables

Modification:
    Add coconut milk to the fried rice as it's cooking in the wok for a whole new flavor.

PORK ADOBO STREET TACOS

Pork shoulder
Soy sauce
White vinegar
Garlic
Sugar
Salt
Bay leaves
Water
Corn or flour tortillas

NOTES

Pineapple salsa

- Slow braise pork shoulder in soy, vinegar, garlic, sugar, salt, bay leaves, and water
- Cook at 275 for 3-4 hours (less about 1-2 hours if using chicken thighs)
- Shred the pork and pile onto the tortillas with salsa

My roommate in grad school, Cecile, is Filipino, so when her mom came to visit one year from Virginia, she made us adobo and lumpia. I took that memory and turned it into adobo street tacos.

Modification:
Serve over rice or cauliflower rice for an entree dish.
If you are using chicken, slow-cook the thighs the same way.

PORK CHOPS, BREADED

Pork chops
Panko
Olive oil
Salt
Pepper

NOTES

- Pat dry pork chops and season with salt and pepper
- Bread with the panko and bake at 375 degrees for 30-35 minutes until internal temperature reaches 145 degrees

Serve with fresh sautéed vegetables and a starch of your choice. The apple chutney pairs well with this also.

PORK STEAKS

Quarter inch-cut shoulder blade steaks
Salt
Pepper
BBQ sauce of your choice

NOTES

- Pull pork steaks out 1 hour prior to grilling to get to room temperature
- Season with salt and pepper
- Make sure the grill is hot and the grates are oiled
- Grill 3-4 minutes then flip
- Apply the first baste of BBQ sauce
- After another 3-4 minutes, flip again
- Apply the second baste to the other side
- I like to baste them and flip them about 4-5 times once the sauce goes on
- About every 1.5 minutes, flip and baste so you start to get caramelization on each side

I also personally like burnt ends, so a little char on the fatty parts of the steak ends up being the best part.

If you want less char, just flip and baste twice and call it a day.

Serve with Mom's potato salad and baked beans.

This is a St. Louis staple and when I lived in San Francisco I couldn't find pork steaks for the life of me. Usually, they are in every grocery store back home, but not out west. My Seester was also out in the Bay Area, and she would have the same issue. So, we found a butcher.

PORK TENDERLOIN

Pork tenderloin
Brown sugar
Garlic
Lemon
Soy or coconut aminos
White wine vinegar
Ground mustard
powder
Olive oil

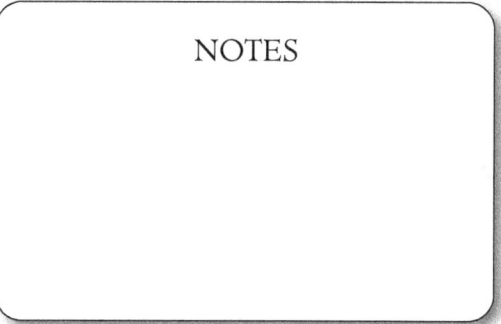

NOTES

- Mix the ingredients together and slather over tenderloin
- Roast at 425 degrees for 25-30 minutes
- Finish the tenderloin by searing on the grill for 2-3 minutes each side
- Let rest about 5-10 minutes
- Slice and serve

Options:
You can also use the same herb mixture and process I use for a whole roasted chicken. This also became the genesis for creating my new Chef Tara's Herb Spice Mix.

Serve over rice with green beans

Serve with roasted potatoes and asparagus or Brussels sprouts

PORTOBELLO STEAK

Portobello mushrooms
Spinach
Panko
Greek yogurt
Mayo
Artichoke hearts
Parmesan
Olive oil
Salt
Pepper

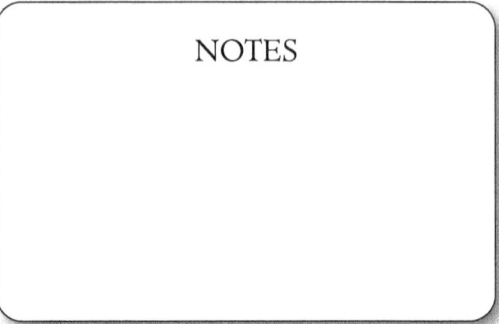

NOTES

- Preheat the oven to 400 degrees
- Clean the large mushroom caps by scraping the "gills" out of the inside then oil and season
- On a baking sheet, cook off the mushroom caps for about 10 minutes until they begin to soften then set aside
- Blanch the spinach and strain, pushing all the water out
- Make the filling by combining spinach with the rest of the ingredients
- Fill the mushroom caps with the spinach mixture
- Bake at 400 degrees for about 10 more minutes until the cheese is melty on top

POT PIE

Frozen mixed vegeta-
bles or fresh corn, peas,
green beans, carrots
Butter
Flour
Stock
Ground chicken or
turkey
Salt
Pepper
Pie crust

NOTES

- In a pot, brown ground chicken
- Add vegetables and cook until tender
- Add butter and flour to create a roux
- Add stock and stir to create a sauce consistency and season to taste
- Pour into pie crust
- Create a topping with a second pie crust with the edges cut off
- Bake at 350 degrees for 45-50 minutes

Modification:

If using fresh vegetables, cut to size then sauté until tender

Make it a Mexican-style pot pie for something different! Use ground beef, tomato soup, corn, black beans, diced chiles, and cheese. Cook all the ingredients in a pot, finishing at the end with the cheese then pouring into a round casserole dish and topping with the pie crust.

PULLED PORK

Pork shoulder roast
BBQ rub
BBQ sauce (use your
favorite brand or make
your own)

I don't use crock pots
often, but for this
dish I do.

- Cut pork shoulder roast into large cubes
- Season with a BBQ rub
- Add BBQ sauce
- Put everything into the crockpot and let it cook all day on low (6-8 hours)

Serve with hamburger buns and creamy coleslaw.

RAMEN

Pork belly (Chashu:
Japanese braised pork
belly)
Hard-boiled eggs
Ramen noodles
Shitake mushrooms
Radishes
Scallions
Chicken broth
Nori seaweed
Dried bonito flakes
Chili oil

The Marinade:
Shoyu
Mirin
Rice vinegar
Sugar
Brown sugar

In order to make sure I had all the different steps I needed, I found a few great Ramen ideas to give me an idea of what all goes into it.

- Make the marinade consisting of the soy, mirin, rice vinegar, and sugars
- Slice hard-boiled eggs and marinate for at least an hour, but a day is even better
- Marinate the pork belly as well for a day
- Begin making the stock by simmering the broth with mushrooms, kelp, and the nori that has been cut into strips
- Strain and keep the stock in the pot simmering on low
- Roast the pork belly at 450 degrees for 30 minutes
- Lower the temperature to 275 and continue to cook for another hour
- Boil noodles and then begin to build your bowl:
  - Noodles
  - Radishes, sliced
  - Pork belly
  - Eggs
  - Mushrooms
  - Broth

RISOTTO

Arborio rice
Chicken stock
White wine
Butter
Parmesan

Options:
Scallops
Asparagus
Peas
Shrimp
Mushrooms

NOTES

Risotto is a labor of love, patience, stirring, and perception of liquid absorption. Once you master the basic risotto, the options are limitless.

- Get two pots going on the stove. One for the 4-ish quarts of stock and the other for the rice dish
- Using a Dutch oven, add the butter and rice, stirring to coat and sauté, about 2 minutes
- Slowly start adding the stock, one ladle at a time until the liquid absorbs
- Stir and stir some more, continuing to ladle in the stock when the liquid is all absorbed
- This will take about 30-40 minutes, tasting the rice until it gets just about al dente

- At this point, add the salt and the cup of white wine, stirring until absorbed
- Finish with butter and parmesan

I was in New York City one year around Thanksgiving visiting my then girlfriend who was from there. We had been dating since meeting at Women's Weekend in Guerneville, CA, on the Russian River that May. A true New Yorker, she was just starting her externship at The French Laundry, a Thomas Keller restaurant. Yes, she was on the culinary path before me, and her name was... Tara. We dated all that summer and so we headed to New York for the holiday. She took me to one of her favorite restaurants, and the risotto had come highly recommended. I had never had anything like it. Pomegranate in risotto! A bit of lemon and asparagus. It was amazing.

Because we were both named Tara, my friends took to calling her Cooking Tara...and that's where and how my website got its name. She was the one following her passion well before me and she inspired me to really think about what and where I wanted to be. When the time came for me to take the leap to culinary school, I called her for advice.

She ended up moving back to New York later that year to work in operations at Per Se, Thomas Keller's new restaurant in New York. Thus, the relationship ended, but the friendship still lives on. We had a great time while we could, and I still look to her for guidance on occasion.

ROASTED CHICKEN OR WOOD-FIRED OVEN CHICKEN

We have a fun, outdoor, wood-fired pizza oven.

Last summer I did a bunch of trial runs with the pizza dough and the firing of the pizza. Some made a mess, others turned out ok. I had issues. I needed to keep practicing.

My favorite pizza place is Ken's Artisan Pizza in Portland, OR. If you didn't get there by about 4:00, you didn't get a seat at the 25-top and there was always a line out the door. This amazing place is the brainchild of Ken Forkish, who much like me, left Silicon Valley and moved to Portland, OR. He wanted to be a baker, I wanted to be a chef.

When it came time to test my hand with the new pizza oven, I immediately consulted his fantastic book *Flour Water Salt Yeast* (2012).

Since my pizza-making skills were not up to par yet, I started using the wood-fired oven for other things, such as a whole chicken. I did some research and found this idea for the chicken on the Fontana oven website.

Whole chicken
Rosemary
Sage
Parsley
Garlic
Salt
Pepper
Olive oil
Butter
Lemon juice

NOTES

- You can either pulse all the herbs with olive oil in a blender or use a mortar and pestle to grind up the herbs then add olive oil, salt, and pepper
- Butter entire chicken
- Spread fresh herb rub over the chicken

- In the wood-fired oven, roast at 440 degrees for 20-25 minutes uncovered
- Baste with the juices in the pan and cover with aluminum foil, maintain heat, and continue to cook until internal temp is 165 degrees, about another hour
- In a conventional oven, simply roast at 350 degrees for 1.5 hours, uncovered

SALMON

Salmon
Olive oil
Salt
Pepper (or Chef Tara's Spice Mix)

NOTES

We eat a lot of salmon at the house, and it's a favorite of the three-year-old. We have it shipped in monthly straight from the waters of Alaska from Custom Seafoods.

I roast it in the oven at 425 degrees for 8-10 minutes until the internal temperature is 125 degrees.

Make sure to check for bones before serving.

Modification:
Add lemon slices on top of the filet while cooking.

Sauté lemon slices in butter and fresh dill to make a simple sauce to pour over the salmon and finish the dish.

Break salmon down to make tacos with an Asian slaw of cabbage and carrots.

Miso-glazed salmon

Salmon poke bowl

Form the salmon into patties by combining it with some Dijon mustard, shallots, and breadcrumbs and sautéing in a skillet or grilling them.

SCALLOPS

Scallops
Salt
Pepper
Paprika
Butter
Grapeseed oil

NOTES

Scallops are a favorite dish at the household, and I have prepared them numerous ways. Scallops live in shells like oysters, clams, and mussels. Most often, when purchasing, you will find scallops already shucked and in two sizes. There are the smaller bay scallops and the larger sea scallops. Before preparation, simply rinse them under running water and remove the hard, little white muscle. It's an oblong tissue that is easy to either cut or pull off.

The most common way to cook scallops is to simply sear them in olive oil or butter. Once you pat them dry, season them on both sides and sear over medium to high heat for about 2-3 minutes each side. You want to get a nice brown crust to develop, which it does very quickly.

Once you have your seared scallops, you can plate them with pasta or over polenta with a side vegetable, such as asparagus.

Another option I like to do is to stir-fry them in a hot wok. Using grapeseed oil, I season the scallops and then cook them over high heat for about 3-4 minutes then set aside and add seasonal vegetables to serve with noodles or rice. Finish with an Asian sauce and you have yet another meal option.

SEA BASS OR HALIBUT

Olive oil
Salt
Pepper

NOTES

- Season filet with salt and pepper and drizzle with olive oil
- Cook at 400 degrees for 12-15 minutes until internal temperature is 135 degrees

Serve as a whole filet over rice or polenta.

Modification:

Flake the filet into pieces for fish tacos with a pineapple or mango salsa.

Add the filet or flaked pieces to any salad for a healthy lunch or dinner option.

SHEPHERD'S PIE

Ground beef
Mixed vegetables (frozen bag works great)
Butter
Flour
Chicken or beef stock
Heavy cream
Salt
Pepper (or Chef Tara's Spice Mix)
Chives
Russet potatoes

NOTES

- Preheat oven to 400 degrees
- Brown ground beef seasoned with salt and pepper and set aside
- Add butter to the pot then add vegetables and sauté
- Add flour to thicken
- Add beef stock to make it saucy but not too soupy
- Boil potatoes
- Add heavy cream, butter, salt, and pepper, and then mash
- In a casserole dish, add the vegetable mix first
- Top with ground beef
- Finish with mashed potatoes
- Bake uncovered at 400 degrees for 25-30 minutes
- Garnish with chives

SHORT RIB RAGU

Beef short ribs
Red wine
Beef stock
Carrots
Celery
Onion
Flour
Tomato paste
Salt
Pepper
Oil

NOTES

- Season short ribs and using a Dutch oven, sear the ribs about 5-6 minutes each side and set aside
- Sauté the mirepoix (carrots, celery, onion)
- Add garlic
- Add flour
- Add red wine
- Add beef stock
- Put the ribs back into the pot
- Cover and slow braise at 325 degrees for 3-3.5 hours

- Pull meat from the bones and let sauce thicken on the stove top
- Serve over polenta or use the meat for tasty short rib tacos with an Asian slaw in soft tortillas

SICHUAN PORK

Ground pork
Sichuan peppercorns
Soy sauce
Peanut oil
Garlic
Ginger
Scallions
Tahini
Chili oil
Chicken stock
Chinese egg noodles or udon noodles

NOTES

- Boil noodles and set aside
- In a wok, toast the peppercorns and set aside for the garnish
- Use a mortar and pestle to grind the peppercorns down
- Sauté the pork in the oil until it is deep fried and set aside
- Stir-fry garlic, ginger, and scallions
- Add soy sauce, tahini, and chili oil
- Add chicken stock and simmer about 4 minutes
- Add pork back to the wok
- Pour over noodles
- Garnish with peppercorns

I found this recipe in Amanda Hesser's new tomb of a cookbook, *The Essential NY Times Cookbook,* and it's a gem. Originally published ten years prior, Hesser updated the cookbook with 120 new recipes in this new "Bible" of American cooking with over 1,000 recipes. I have used it frequently for inspiration and ideas and challenged myself to cook as many of the recipes as I could during my tenure with my client.

SLOPPY JOE, AKA THE SPOON BURGER

This was a personal request one week from my client when I asked her what she was craving. She said, "the spoon burger," the good, old childhood favorite, Sloppy Joe. She hadn't had it since she was a kid, and to be honest, neither had I, so I was more than happy to revisit this memorable dish. She told me how her mom used to make it, then she would sneak in the kitchen and add more brown sugar, as she liked it sweeter. So, I texted her mother and got a simple text back:

No recipe
(shrug emoji)
Onion
Chopped peppers
(green pepper emoji)
Ketchup
Brown sugar with a
little BBQ sauce
Salt & pepper
Think kid-friendly,
not spicy
more sweet
Quick & easy

NOTES

- Begin by sautéing the onions and peppers then add in the ground beef
- Once the ground beef is properly browned, add in the ketchup, brown sugar, and a little BBQ sauce of your choice
- Add more brown sugar if you like it sweeter, as we did, and finish with some salt and pepper
- Serve in buns and call it a day

Oh, and chips...you need potato chips with this meal.

SMASH BURGERS

Ground beef
Chef Tara's Spice Mix
American cheese
Secret sauce

NOTES

- Season ground
  beef with salt
  and pepper
- Make your beef
  into just a bit
  bigger than golf ball sized balls
- On a flat-top or cast-iron skillet, sear the beef using a spatula to push flat
- Flip once after 2-3 minutes and top with American cheese
- Toast brioche bun on the skillet
- Build your burger
- Double it up
- Sauce it up

In & Out is my favorite, Shake Shack a close second, though that came later in life. I lived with In & Out for twenty-plus years while in San Francisco, and it was glorious. Double-Double Animal Style is my jam. IYKYK

So now that I am back in the Midwest and burger-less, I had to create a somewhat similar option for the family and my own enjoyment.

By 2023, smash burgers had become the new foodie buzz word dish. I've been making them before they were cool.

SPAGHETTI NIGHT WITH GARLIC BREAD

Spaghetti noodles
Ground beef
Tomato sauce
Tomato paste
Salt
Pepper (or Chef Tara's
Spice Mix)

NOTES

- Boil noodles
- Brown
  ground beef
- Add tomato sauce and tomato paste
- Season with spices
- Let simmer about 25-30 minutes

Growing up, spaghetti night was a gourmet meal, and it consisted of a jar of Ragu and tomato paste. Mom would add a little dash of oregano, and it was like going to Olive Garden. In that moment, it was the best spaghetti we ever had. I think my Seester still makes it exactly the same way, as one should.

SPATCHCOCK CHICKEN

Use the same technique and seasoning as roasted chicken. This will cut the cooking time down and is a cool presentation. Also, it's easier to get into a wood-fired oven.

Cut the breastbone in half and lay the chicken flat

NOTES

Every August there are eight of us former college volley-ball teammates that converge on Long Beach, IN, for our yearly reunion. We have been connected through volleyball for over thirty years. One of Jen's specialties is the spatchcock chicken, so a few summers ago we grabbed two whole chickens, I made her show me her tips and tricks, so I could menu it for the house.

- Put the chicken skin-side up on the grill on the indirect side of the grill
- Turn off the middle burner while the rest of the burners are at medium-high heat
- For a charcoal grill, move the charcoal to one side of the grill and put the chicken on the other side
- Cover and cook until the internal temperature is 150-160 degrees (approx. 30-40 minutes)
- Move the chicken to the direct heat for 2 minutes
- Flip the chicken to sear the skin side and get a nice char for about 3-4 minutes
- The chicken is done when the internal temperature has reached 165 degrees
- Serve over mixed greens or arugula

STEAKS

Ribeye or your favor-ite cut
Salt
Pepper
Olive oil

NOTES

Find a friend (THANK YOU DEBBIE) who sells cows and buy your own half or whole cow for the best steaks you will ever have. In my opinion.

Ribeye is the favorite cut around this house.

We bought a half cow the first year, and it fits with room to spare in a stand-up freezer. So, for the second year, we are upgrading to the whole kit and kaboodle. Remember Caboodles? You were hip and cool back in the 1980s if you had one of these. Now I am dating myself. The origin of it is a funny story. Apparently back in 1986, Vanna White was photographed using a Plano fishing tackle box to store her makeup. Well, Plano fishing tackle company thought ahead, and the rest is history. SQUIRREL...ok, where were we?

Yes, steak...here we go.

- Take your steak out of the fridge about 2 hours before cooking
- Let it get to room temp
- Keep it simple
- Salt and pepper (I often use my spice mix as well)
- Use just a drizzle of oil on each side, which I find helps it keep from sticking to the grill
- Grill flipping only once
- Cook about 4 minutes per side for medium rare
- Let it rest for about 15 minutes before slicing it, per Seester

STEAK TEMPS:
Rare 125 degrees F, 52 degrees C
Medium Rare 135 degrees F, 57 degrees C
Medium 145 degrees F, 63 degrees C
Medium Well 150 degrees F, 66 degrees C
Well done...REALLY? I can't.

STIR-FRY

Chicken, steak, or
shrimp
Snow peas
Peppers
Broccoli
Cauliflower
Pineapple
Everyday Asian sauce

NOTES

This is an "all the kids
in the pool" dish...use a hot wok and toss everything in quickly
until the proteins are cooked to temperature.

Finish dish with a quick toss in the sauce the last minute or two
of cooking.

Plate over rice, cauliflower rice, or noodles.

Super healthy, super quick, and easy.

SUMMER PASTA

Linguini
Asparagus
Zucchini
Peas
Olive oil
Garlic
Lemon juice
Salt
Pepper (or Chef Tara's
Spice Mix)

NOTES

This is a light, fun dish for the hot summer nights in the Midwest.

- Simply cook off the pasta of your choice and toss with sautéed vegetables
- Finish with a garlic-infused olive oil and a few squeezes of fresh lemon
- Serve with garlic naan on the grill and a nice salad

TACO NIGHT

Hard-shell tacos
Shredded iceberg
lettuce
Tomatoes
Ground beef
Shredded cheese blend
(cheddar and colby)
Sour cream
Cholula

NOTES

Taco Seasoning:
Chef Tara's Spice mix
Chili powder
Cumin

The tacos that you just can't help but eat three, four, or ten. When I was in college, my nickname was "Chubby," not because I was overweight, quite the opposite. I was about 5'8" and 120 pounds, and I could eat a lot of food when my volleyball teammates couldn't. But that is a whole therapy session. To this day, my college pals and their children still call me "Aunt Chubby." So back in the day, Taco Bell had a ten-pack party pack of hard-shell tacos. I was challenged to eat them all in one sitting. I did.

There is nothing like homemade, old-school, hard-shell tacos.

You know what to do…brown the ground beef, add the seasoning, and go to town.

TERIYAKI CHICKEN

Chicken thighs
Soy
Brown sugar
Garlic
Ginger
Cinnamon
Salt
Pepper

NOTES

- Season chicken thighs with salt and pepper
- Combine the rest of the ingredients in a pot to make a sauce
- Cook chicken at 425 degrees for 15 minutes
- Baste chicken with sauce and cook for 5 minutes
- Baste again and finish cooking the chicken until it reaches an internal temp of 165 degrees
- Baste again before serving

Modification:
Serve over rice or cauliflower rice
Serve with sautéed vegetables
Pour sauce over the dish

TUNA POKE BOWL

Raw sushi grade tuna
Soy sauce
Sesame oil
Pineapple
Mango
Edamame
Cucumber
Scallion
Mayo and
Sriracha sauce
Sesame seeds

NOTES

- Dice the tuna and let soak for 30 minutes or longer in the soy sauce and sesame oil
- Add any ingredient combination you like to the bowl of rice and top with the tuna
- Garnish with sesame seeds
- Serve over rice or cauliflower rice
- Serve with Poke sauce

Modification:
Salmon

Poke originates from the Hawaii islands, and is a simple yet delicious dish of diced raw fish marinated in a variety of seasonings, such as soy sauce, sesame oil, and green onions.

Kauai, HI, is one of my favorite places on earth. I have been numerous times, and essentially it is where I first had poke. Pono Market in Kapaa

on Kauai was a place I would frequent. The fish is so incredibly fresh and delicious. The island is a happy place for me that instills a calmness within. Poke bowls are the perfect refresher on a hot day, and a perfect meal any time. So anytime I can make these, it takes me right back to Hawaii.

VEAL MARSALA

Veal
Salt
Pepper
Flour
Olive oil
Marsala wine
Mushrooms
Chicken stock
Thyme
Butter

NOTES

- Season veal
- Dredge veal in flour
- Add to a sauté pan with hot oil
- Cook 2-4 minutes each side
- Remove from heat and set aside on a rack or plate
- Add marsala wine, scraping crunchy bits off the pan
- Add mushrooms
- Season as you go, so add some salt to the mushrooms
- Add stock and fresh thyme
- Reduce liquid by half
- Return veal to the pan, spooning liquid over the veal until heated through
- Plate veal, then add butter to the sauce to finish and pour over the veal

VIETNAMESE SHAKING BEEF

Beef cubed
Rice vinegar
Sugar
Soy
Fish sauce
Garlic
Salt
Pepper

NOTES

- Mix all ingredients and toss with the beef in a hot skillet
- That's it
- Really
- I promise
- Serve over arugula or any leafy green

Chef Charles Phan created this dish at the Slanted Door in San Francisco, and it's one of his most famous dishes.

When I first moved to San Francisco in 1993 for grad school, Slanted Door was this little restaurant in the Mission that just served great food. Now it's an over 8,000-square-foot spot on the waterfront in the Ferry Building that is a tourist favorite and a local staple.

CHAPTER 11

THE SIDES

"Mussels, it's so nice to see you again."

AMISH NOODLES

Egg noodles
Beef stock
Salt

My Grandma Walton used to make this when she served us her famous roast beef dinner. My grandparents lived in Sullivan, IL, which was close to Arthur, IL, and home to a large Amish community. They had a cleaning lady, Ann Marie, who was the only Amish person I had ever met. I assumed that's where Grandma got the noodles, since they were called "Amish noodles." I was just a kid and didn't know any the wiser, but they were delicious and I never forgot them.

- Generously add salt to beef stock and bring to a boil
- Add the egg noodles and cook on high heat then lower to a simmer and let the noodles soak up the beef stock

APPLE CHUTNEY

Honeycrisp apples
Brown sugar
Apple juice
Cinnamon
Lemon juice

- Dice apples and add all ingredients to the pot
- Bring to a boil
- Let simmer about 1-2 hours until the apples start to break down but still chunky
- Watch the level of the liquid and add more apple juice so it doesn't dry out

This is great served over pork chops.
I got this idea from Rae Drummond's recipe for a simple apple sauce.

ASIAN SLAW

Red cabbage
Carrots
Scallions
Thai chili sauce
Rice wine vinegar

- Slice red cabbage and carrots into thin strips
- Slice the scallions on the bias
- Toss with the Thai chili sauce and rice wine vinegar

AU GRATIN POTATOES

Russet or Yukon gold potatoes
Butter
Flour
Milk
Shredded cheddar cheese
Gruyere
Salt
Pepper (or Chef Tara's Spice Mix)

This is a favorite often requested. I love these a lot too. My mom used to make these all the time, but it was the Betty Crocker box with the potatoes in a bag and the potatoes were little potato chip things. She'd pour it in a pot, add the powdered stuff, and magically they would become deliciousness.

- Preheat oven to 400 degrees
- Thinly slice potatoes with a mandolin
- Layer the potatoes in a casserole dish
- Make the roux: equal parts butter and flour
- Add milk to create the sauce (which is a béchamel)
- Add cheese (presto, you have a mornay sauce)

- Pour cheese sauce over potatoes
- Top with more shredded cheese
- Bake for 1-1.5 hours

AVOCADO SALSA

Avocado
Red onion
Red pepper
Corn
Lime juice
Salt

- You can use canned corn, but better yet, blanch some fresh corn from the farmer's market then cut the kernels off the cob
- Dice the avocado, red onion, and red pepper
- Toss all ingredients together with lime juice and add some salt

BAKED BEANS

Pinto beans
Navy beans
BBQ sauce

I have made some baked bean dishes before that take hours to make, but since time is limited sometimes, I came up with this quick and easy one.

Cook the canned beans in your favorite barbecue sauce and call it a day.

If you want to get fancy, cook off some bacon and onions in the pot, add the beans, then add the sauce.

BAKED POTATO

Russet potato
Olive oil
Salt
Pepper

We often did a baked potato bar for lunchtime meals. I personally love them, and it makes a full meal for me with just some butter and cottage cheese. Yes, cottage cheese, not sour cream for me. Try it sometime!

- Slather baked potato in olive oil then generously cover with salt and pepper
- Roast in the oven at 425 degrees for about an hour
- Stick a fork in them to test for doneness

The skin should be nice and crispy.

For our baked potato bar, I always had crispy bacon, chives, sour cream, and cheddar cheese available.

CAULIFLOWER STEAKS

Cauliflower
Olive oil
Salt
Pepper (or Chef Tara's Spice Mix)

- Cut the whole head of the cauliflower top down to stem so the slices stay together and replicate a flat steak
- Season with oil and spices
- Roast at 425 degrees for 20-25 minutes

CHEF TARA'S SPRINGROLL MASHUP

Rice paper wrapper
Rice noodles
Cucumber
Carrot
Mint
Red cabbage

Mango Salsa:
Parsley
Mango
Red pepper
Red onion
Lime juice
Salt
Soba sauce for dipping

This is a fun mashup that occurred one day in the kitchen. I had leftover mango salsa from the night before but wanted to make some spring rolls for lunch. So, I took the normal ingredients in a spring roll, the cucumber, carrot, cabbage, and mint, but I added the mango salsa to it. When I say it was one of the best things I have tasted, I wasn't exaggerating. The combination of all the flavors was amazing, mixed with the soba dipping sauce.

The key to this is the julienne cut of the cucumber, cabbage, red pepper, and red onion. You want nice long slices of each so they fit nicely in the wrapper.

- Wet the rice paper rounds in water until they are pliable
- Cook off the rice noodles to the package specifications, cool, and set aside
- Lay the rice paper on a clean cutting board and layer all the ingredients

- Fold the wrapper in on the left and right sides then roll it all together
- Slice in half and enjoy with the soba dipping sauce

You're welcome.

CORNBREAD

Cornmeal
Buttermilk
Flour
Baking powder
Baking salt
Salt
Egg

- Mix all the ingredients, wet together and dry together, then combine
- Pour into an 8" x 8" pan and bake at 400 degrees for about 25-30 minutes

This recipe is typically on the cornmeal package so you can follow that as well.

FRUIT JAM

Bananas, blueberries, strawberries
Lemon juice
Sugar

- Slice the fruit (or keep blueberries whole) and add to a pot with the lemon juice and about a cup of sugar
- Let simmer on low until the sugar has dissolved
- Use a potato masher to break up the mixture
- Taste for sweetness and add more sugar if desired

GARLIC BREAD

Sourdough bread
Garlic
Butter
Chef Tara's Spice Mix

- Melt butter with minced garlic and spice mix
- Baste onto the bread
- Bake at 425 degrees for 8-10 minutes

Modification:
We use naan quite a bit and this makes a great substitution instead of bread.

GRILLED OR ROASTED VEGETABLES

Asparagus
Brussels sprouts
Zucchini
Squash
Olive oil
Salt
Pepper (or Chef Tara's Spice Mix)

Keep it simple.

Prep vegetables:

- Trim asparagus
- Halve or quarter Brussels sprouts
- Slice zucchini and squash
- Toss with olive oil and seasoning

Grill:

- Asparagus: 4-5 minutes
- Brussels sprouts: 8-10 minutes
- Carrots: 5-6 minutes
- Squash: 5-6 minutes
- Zucchini: 5-6 minutes

Roast at 425 degrees:

- Asparagus: 6-8 minutes
- Brussels sprouts: 25-30 minutes
- Carrots: 15-20 minutes
- Squash: 15-20 minutes
- Zucchini: 15-20 minutes

It is much easier to grill vegetables as whole as possible, so by just cutting them in half or quarters, you can cook them directly on the grates of the grill simply with olive oil and spices. Then you can cut them down to the size you need for whatever dish it is you are making.

Modification:
Glaze carrots or Brussels sprouts with honey before roasting to create a sweet side dish.

GIARDINIERA

Cauliflower
Celery
Carrot
Red bell pepper
Green olives
Serrano pepper
Garlic clove

Pickling Liquid:
White wine vinegar
Water
Kosher salt
Coriander seed
Yellow mustard seed
Fennel seed
Black peppercorns
Celery seeds
Bay leaf
oregano

For Chicago-Style Relish:
White vinegar
Olive oil
Grapeseed oil
Salt
Garlic
Oregano
Red pepper flakes
Celery seed
Black peppercorns

To make a classic giardiniera, whether you are pickling it or making it like a Chicago-style relish for an Italian beef sandwich, your vegetables need to be diced up small enough to fit on said sandwiches. Not as small as the olive tapenade we use on the muffuletta. Just nice bite-size pieces of all the vegetables.

Bring vinegar to a boil with all the ingredients, let cool, then pour over the small, diced vegetables in a Ball jar.

Let sit for at least 24 hours before serving.

GUACAMOLE

- Avocados, 2-3
- A generous spoonful of Chef Tara's Spice Mix
- Squeeze of half a lime or lemon

Literally, that's it.

HOMEMADE POTATO CHIPS

Russet potatoes
Olive oil
Salt

- Use a mandolin to thinly slice the potatoes
- Toss with olive oil and seasonings
- Bake at 425 degrees about 8-10 minutes

HOMEMADE TORTILLA CHIPS

Corn or flour tortillas
Olive oil
Salt

- Use a pizza cutter and cut into triangles
- Season with oil and salt
- Bake at 375 degrees for 8 minutes then flip
- Cook for 4 minutes then flip once more
- Total cook time about 14-16 minutes

MAC AND CHEESE

Elbow macaroni noodles
Gruyere cheese
Cheddar cheese
Heavy cream
Salt
Pepper
Nutmeg

Ina Garten, in her newest cookbook, changed my life. I am a religious *TODAY Show* watcher, and every morning it is on. One morning, Ina was promoting her new cookbook, *Go-To-Dinners: A Barefoot Contessa Cookbook,* and she made her new overnight mac and cheese. I literally stopped in my tracks and thought, "Oh, my God, no more roux…no more flour!"

This was a game changer and my new go-to recipe for all things mac and cheese.

Cook the pasta and when it's done, add it to a large bowl with the rest of the ingredients.

Cover it and put it in the refrigerator for 24 hours. This allows the pasta to soak up the sauce.

The next day put it into a casserole dish, top with more Gruyere and cheddar cheese, and bake at 400 degrees for 20-25 minutes.

Ina tops hers with breadcrumbs. You either like breadcrumbs on your mac and cheese, or you don't. You do you.

MANGO SALSA

Mango
Red onion
Red bell pepper
Salt
Lime juice
Cilantro

- Dice mango, red onion, and red bell pepper
- Add to a bowl and toss with lime juice, salt, and pepper
- Add cilantro at the end if you like it, or you can use parsley for the color

MOM'S BROCCOLI CHEESE CASSEROLE

I am putting this in just because I can. Because it's one of my first memories of Mom passing on a recipe to my Seester and I. I don't think I have ever had a Thanksgiving without it. I will make it and take wherever I go, if possible, whether it is on the menu or not. And if I can't have it where I am attending, then I just make it for myself and eat it for a week. It has all the processed cheesy good-ness that is Cheese Whiz and Velveeta because why not? And of course you can substitute and "Chef It Up" like my friend's kids always warned me about NOT doing, by adding fancy cheese, fresh broccoli, and a nice basmati rice. Heck, you can even make your own cream of chicken soup if you want to go crazy. I mean, why not churn your own butter? But why would you when Mom knows best? Just go with it and enjoy.

Frozen chopped broccoli
Cream of chicken soup
Cheese Whiz
Butter
Minute rice

Velveeta cheese
Salt
Pepper

I am copying this word for word per Mom. This is the only idea with exact amounts because you should make it exactly like Mom did.

- Preheat oven to 350 degrees
- Add ½ cup water in saucepan
- Add ¼ cup butter—heat
- Add broccoli—heat and stir for 5 minutes until warm
- Add 2 cups minute rice
- Add 2 cups cream of chicken soup
- Add ½ cup water
- Add Cheese Whiz
- Add salt and pepper
- Spray casserole dish
- Top with Velveeta
- Heat at 350 degrees for 35-40 minutes, when it gets bubbly around the edges

And scene...

Broccoli Casserole

Always in the market for—
NEWS

1 C. (un cooked) minute rice
1 C. celery
1 onion ⎬ cook until tender
3/4 stick oleo

(2) 1 pkg. frozen broccoli Add 1/2 C. water. Add to celery & onion & cook 5 minutes. Add 1 small jar Cheese Whiz. 1 Can cream of chicken soup & uncooked rice (add about 1/2 C. more water.)

Bake 25 min. at 350.°

* If only use 1 box broccoli, don't add last 1/2 C. water. Velveeta cheese too. 2 boxes makes it thicker. 2 soup / 2 C. rice – more water if needed

151

MOM'S POTATO SALAD

Yukon gold potatoes	Yellow mustard
Hard-boiled eggs	Salt
Sweet pickles	Pepper
Mayo	

I asked my Seester to send me the recipe for this since she makes it all the time. I know I should have it written down somewhere, but I literally couldn't find it. So, I sent her a text and this is what I got (I am keeping this in its original format because it's just too funny):

"Heading to Palm Springs this morning. It's one thing I don't have a recipe for.

Here's the scoop—

Peel and cube potatoes (russet), about 1" pieces.

Boil until tender but not mushy.

Drain and spread on baking sheet to cool.

I don't wait for them to cool completely.

I buy pre-made hard-boiled eggs now.

Cut them up.

Slice sweet pickles (I use a lot of egg and pickle cuz it makes me happy).

The sauce—lots of mayo, yellow mustard, dijon mustard, pickle juices, salt/pepper.

Mix and add as needed.

I like lots of sauce. It makes me happy!

There is some speculation that Mom used Miracle Whip not mayo.

I add a scoop or two for tang.

Cool.

Adjust to your happiness" – Marnie Triefenbach Herrling, text message 3/9/2023 10:31 a.m.

We lost our mom rather quickly to pancreatic cancer. It came quick and suddenly before we even knew what the hell was happening. This recipe is near and dear to both of our hearts. Treat it well.

POLENTA

Polenta
Water
Butter
Parmesan cheese
Salt

I love Bob's Red Mill products from Oregon. The facility where all this is made is not far from where I went to culinary school. Whatever brand you use, the instructions are on the packaging and will help guide you through making this dish. Check the ratio of water to polenta. It's usually 2:1, sometimes 4:1.

- Bring the water and salt to a boil and add the polenta, stirring to avoid lumps
- Reduce the heat to low and let simmer for about 30 minutes, checking every few minutes or so with a good stir
- Turn off the heat and add in the butter and the cheese and continue stirring until the cheese has melted

Serve immediately.

PICO SALSA

Tomato
Onion
Jalapeno
Cilantro
Salt
Lime juice

- Dice tomato, onion, and jalapeño and add to a bowl
- Toss with cilantro, lime juice, and salt

PICKLED RED ONIONS

Red onion
Red wine
Red wine vinegar
Salt
Sugar

- Slice red onions and put them in a quart-size Ball jar
- Bring to a boil equal parts red wine and red wine vinegar, depending on how many onions you are pickling, with 2:1 ratio of sugar to salt
- Example: (4 cups each of wine and vinegar, 2 cups sugar, 1 cup salt)
- Let cool, then pour over sliced red onions
- Let sit at least 24 hours, preferably a few days before serving

These make a great addition to many dishes and salads for about 2 months.

PINEAPPLE SALSA

Pineapple
Red onion
Red bell pepper
Salt
Lime juice
Cilantro

- Dice pineapple, red onion, and red bell pepper
- Add to a bowl and toss with lime juice, salt, and pepper
- Add cilantro at the end if you like it, or you can use parsley for the color

POMME FRITES (FRENCH FRIES)

Yukon gold potatoes
Olive oil
Salt

- Slice potatoes into French fry size strips and let soak in water as you continue to cut the rest of the potatoes
- Drain the potatoes well and make sure they are nice and dry
- Toss with olive oil and season with salt
- Place them on a well-oiled baking sheet then bake at 450 degrees for 15-20 minutes
- Flip using tongs or a spatula and cook for another 5-10 minutes until they are golden brown and crispy
- Season with more salt or any other seasonings of your choice

A favorite accompaniment to these is Chef Tara's Special Sauce. Dip away!

ROASTED FINGERLING POTATOES

Fingerling potatoes
Olive oil
Salt
Pepper (or Chef Tara's Spice Mix)

- Slice or quarter potatoes
- Toss with olive oil and season with either salt and pepper or Chef Tara's Original Spice Mix
- Bake at 425 degrees for 35-40 minutes until browned and crispy

SAUTÉED GREEN BEANS

Green beans
Soy sauce
Minced garlic
Minced fresh ginger
Red pepper chili flakes
Olive oil

Tip and tail the green beans, as Grandma used to say. When we were kids, as the green beans were picked from the garden, we were tasked with tipping and tailing the green beans in the hot summer sun. In non-grandma speak, you take the ends off the beans.

I like to blanch my green beans before I sauté them for any dishes.

- Take the green beans and boil them in hot water for about 3 minutes
- "Shock" them with ice cold water to stop the cooking process
- In a hot wok with the oil, add the rest of the ingredients and begin sautéing, quickly tossing the pan frequently to prevent burning

Optional: garnish with sliced almonds or sesame seeds.

SCALLOP ESCABECHE

Raw scallops
Red pepper
Red onion
Lime
Salt

- Dice the scallops, red pepper, and red onion
- Generously squeeze in some fresh lime juice as the acid from the lime juice will cook the scallops
- Let sit in the refrigerator for at least 10 minutes or longer
- Season with salt and serve with your homemade tortilla chips

Escabeche, or ceviche, is literally cooking seafood in lime juice. This can be done with shrimp as well.

SMASHED POTATOES

Yukon gold potatoes
Olive oil
Salt
Pepper (or Chef Tara's Spice Mix)

- Par boil the potatoes in a pot until tender enough to smash
- Using a baking pan, put down parchment paper and spray with olive oil
- Smash each potato until mostly flat using the palm of your hand or the bottom of a pint glass as they will be hot
- Drizzle with olive oil and season
- Bake at 425 degrees for 25-30 minutes until browned and crispy
- Finish with salt

Get creative! You can turn these into an ultimate smashed potato by adding some bacon, cheese, and chives.

TORTILLA BOWL

Burrito-size flour tortilla
Chef Tara's Spice Mix (or salt works just fine)
Olive oil

- Oil and season the tortilla well
- Use a small to medium glass bowl upside down on a sheet pan
- Put the tortilla over it to form an upside-down bowl
- Cover with aluminum foil
- Bake at 425 degrees for 5 minutes covered
- Remove aluminum foil and bake for another 5 minutes uncovered
- Remove the glass bowl and flip the tortilla over and cook for the final 3 minutes

CHAPTER 12

SOUPS

"I have something very exquisite to show Mama."

WHEN I COOKED AT REED COLLEGE IN PORTLAND, OR, back when I was the first in the kitchen bright and early at 6 a.m., I oversaw making the soups for the day. Three different soups by 11:00 a.m. in two giant kettles that sat about as high as just under my shoulders. My whisk was about four feet long and it was awesome. I had to make a meat soup, a vegetarian soup, and a vegan soup every day, so fifteen soups a week. Boy, was that fun! No really, it was. I worked with such fabulous chefs that the walk-in was full of brilliant and fun ideas for soups. I could use what was left over from the previous night's dinners. We had a vegan chef on staff, so whatever he made the night before, I could pull it and turn it into a delicious soup with some tweaks. The same with the meat-based and the vegetarian. I could use parts of it as a base to start with and then add different ingredients, working off that original flavor profile. I made some pretty kick ass soups that have no names. They aren't duplicated anywhere. One of a kind on that day only if you were lucky.

Since I only had two kettles, I would get the vegan soup going in one and a meat version in the other. The vegan soup usually didn't take long to make since I was working with mostly vegetables so I would pull that one out first, thus freeing up that kettle to then

159

start the vegetarian soup. Once that was done and the meat soup had finished simmering, I would pull those two out at the same time and all three were ready for service. It was like soup Tetris.

So, here's the thing. I have given you some soups that are pretty standard, known to be great soups that I made over the course of that year. But I also took those soups and tweaked and played with them, and I created totally new soups that provide you with yet another idea in your toolbox.

The ingredients are there, and the process is the same, just change up some things. Take out one thing and add two others.

From the always-famous clam chowder, you can take out the clams and clam juice and anything fishy related and:

Add potatoes, bacon, and cheddar cheese and you have a baked potato soup.

Add corn and chicken and you have a creamy corn chicken chowder.

Add chicken and rice and...well, you get the picture.

Same with minestrone, my favorite soup. If you use that as a base and say add chicken and tortillas and different seasonings, well, you get chicken and tortilla soup.

Take out the beans and pasta and you get a straight up vegetable soup.

Add tortellini or chicken and orzo and you get something different yet again.

This goes back to that good old flavor profile! Once you have the base soups conquered, tweak them! Try new things. Add some hot sauce. I dare you.

BROCCOLI CHEDDAR SOUP

Carrot	Cheddar cheese
Onion	Broccoli
Butter	Salt
Flour	Pepper
Milk	

The St. Louis Bread Co., back in the day, made this popular. It was one of my mom's favorite things. This soup and Cheerios were the only things we could get her to eat in the last three months of her life. Needless to say, it brings up memories for me and to this day, and I won't eat it. And for the longest time, I wouldn't even make it. The family I cook for enjoys this soup, so when it was requested one day, of course I obliged. I channeled Mom and made it the best I could with lots of love and patience.

- Sauté diced onion and carrot in butter
- Add flour
- Add milk to make a sauce then more to create a soup consistency
- Add cheddar cheese
- Add broccoli
- Season to taste and let simmer for at least 30 minutes

CLAM CHOWDER

Clams	Flour
Celery	Half and half
Carrots	Milk
Onion	Russet potato
Bacon	Clam juice
Garlic	Salt
Butter	Pepper

We get our clams live from Hog Island Oyster Co., so I will cook a double batch of the clams in the white wine sauce and save some to make this chowder.

- Using the cooked clams, dice and set aside
- If using canned clams, dice as well
- Cook off bacon in the oven, (375 degrees about 35 minutes), dice and set aside
- Sauté mirepoix (carrots, celery, onion) in butter then add garlic
- Stir in flour to create the roux then add half and half to thicken
- Add milk and clam juice to create a soup consistency
- Add diced potatoes and clams and season to taste
- Finally, put the bacon back into the pot and let simmer until potatoes are cooked through, about 25-30 minutes

GROUND TURKEY AND VEGETABLE SOUP

Ground turkey	Chicken stock
Onion	Salt
Carrot	Pepper
Celery	Olive oil
Zucchini	

- In a Dutch oven, add the diced mirepoix (carrots, celery, onion) and sauté in oil
- Brown the ground turkey in the pot with the vegetables
- Add in diced zucchini and chicken stock and season to taste
- Bring to a boil then let simmer until ready to serve

ITALIAN SOUP

Onion	Chicken stock
Carrot	Diced tomato
Celery	Tomato sauce
Asparagus	Orzo
Zucchini	Parmesan
Squash	Salt
Swiss chard	Pepper
Ground pork	

- Brown ground pork and set aside
- Sauté mirepoix (carrots, celery, onion)
- Add rest of vegetables, minus the Swiss chard, and sauté
- Add diced tomatoes
- Add tomato sauce
- Add stock and season to taste
- Return pork back to the pot
- Add pasta if serving immediately to cook in the soup
- Finish with Swiss chard and parmesan, cooking until the Swiss chard is done, about 2 minutes

Modification:

Use ground beef, ground chicken, or ground turkey.

Leave out the protein and use vegetable stock for a vegetarian option.

Cook pasta separately and reserve until serving the soup so it doesn't soak up all the liquid.

LEMON GREEK POTATO SOUP

Celery	Chicken stock
Carrot	Yukon gold potatoes
Onion	Chicken breast
Oregano	Calrose white rice
Dill	Salt
Garlic	Pepper
Lemon juice	Olive oil
Lemon zest	

- Cook off chicken in the oven and set aside
- Small dice mirepoix (carrots, celery, onion) and sauté in olive oil
- Add the garlic
- Add chicken broth and bring to a boil
- Add the rice
- Season to taste
- Simmer until the rice is cooked, about 20 minutes
- Add cooked chicken that has been shredded
- Add lemon juice to finish the dish

MINESTRONE

Celery	Diced tomatoes
Carrot	Vegetable stock (or chicken)
Onion	Kidney beans
Garlic	Rotini pasta (or penne)
Zucchini	Parmesan shredded
Squash	Salt
Green beans	Pepper

At the end of the week, I'll take whatever leftover vegetables I have in the house and turn it into a nice soup for the weekend. Typically,

I have planned for exactly what I need every week, but occasionally, I have some left. Otherwise, I menu this and order accordingly.
This is another "all the kids in the pool" dish.

- In a bit of oil, sauté the mirepoix (carrots, celery, onion)
- Add garlic
- Add rest of vegetables
- Add diced tomatoes
- Add kidney beans
- Cover with stock and season to taste
- Bring to a boil
- Let simmer for 30-60 minutes or longer, depending on when you want to serve
- Cook off pasta separately and set aside
- In a bowl, add the pasta, cover with soup, and top with parmesan
- Serve with crusty bread

I keep the pasta separate so it doesn't soak up all the liquid

Modification:
Add uncooked pasta to soup if serving immediately. The pasta will cook in the soup, just watch your liquid level and add more stock as needed.

MULLIGATAWNY

Chicken thigh	Chicken stock
Apple	Curry powder
Carrot	Salt
Celery	Butter
Onion	Heavy cream
Bay leaf	Greek yogurt

In a pot or Dutch oven, add:

- Diced chicken thighs
- Diced apples and mirepoix (carrots, celery, onion)
- Sauté until chicken is cooked through (165 internal temp.)
- Add curry powder, salt, butter, heavy cream and yogurt
- Fill pot with chicken stock and season to taste
- Bring to a boil and then let simmer for at least an hour so all the flavors meld together

ROASTED CHICKEN NOODLE SOUP

Roast chicken	Salt
Celery	Pepper
Carrot	Italian seasoning
Onion	Oregano
Egg noodles	Olive oil
Chicken stock	

- Sauté the mirepoix (carrots, celery, onion) in olive oil
- Add chicken stock, season, and bring to a boil
- Add the roasted chicken leftovers that have been shredded
- Add the egg noodles and let simmer until the noodles are fully cooked

Modification:

Add seasonal vegetables

Pre-cook the noodles and add when the soup is ready to be served.

Use rice and add heavy cream to make it a creamy chicken and rice soup.

THANKSGIVING TURKEY NOODLE SOUP

Celery	Salt
Carrot	Pepper
Onion	Rosemary
Thanksgiving turkey leftovers	Thyme
Egg noodles	Sage
Chicken stock	Olive oil

- Sauté the mirepoix (carrots, celery, onion) in olive oil
- Add turkey stock, season, and bring to a boil
- Add the Thanksgiving turkey leftovers that have been shredded
- Add the egg noodles and let simmer until the noodles are fully cooked

Modification:

Add seasonal vegetables

Pre-cook the noodles and add when the soup is ready to be served.

CHAPTER 13

SALADS

"Chef Tara, I think you are the Queen of Food."

WHEN I MAKE SALADS, SOMETIMES I GO WITH A classic like Caesar, chef, or cobb. But that's too easy. Oftentimes my client will ask me to try and replicate one that she had enjoyed recently at a restaurant.

Most times I will take stock of what I have on hand and create a salad from those ingredients, making sure that the flavors of everything I put in the bowl will complement each other.

Some of the salads don't really have an exact name, per se, so I named them based on what ingredient stands out the most.

Play around with all of them. Use different dressings or use two. I am notorious for using some ranch and some Italian or balsamic on one salad. I like to mix it up.

ASIAN SALAD

Romaine
Cabbage
Scallions
Almonds
Snow peas

Red peppers
Mandarin oranges
Wonton strips
Asian vinaigrette

AVOCADO SALAD

Avocado
Red onion
Tomato
Mixed baby greens
Lemon vinaigrette

BBQ CHICKEN SALAD

BBQ chicken breast
Romaine
Tomato
Corn
Black beans

Red onion
Monterey jack cheese
Cheddar cheese
Tortilla strips
Ranch dressing

B's FAVORITE FRUIT SALAD

Peach
Apple
Orange
Blueberry
Raspberry
Marcona almonds
Avocado

Blue cheese
Mixed greens
Orange vinaigrette

BRUSSELS SPROUT SALAD

Shredded Brussels sprouts
Arugula
Dried cherries
Apple
Pistachio

Chickpeas
Feta
Mint
Dijon poppy vinaigrette

CHEF TARA'S SALAD

Ham
Turkey
Salami
Provolone

Cheddar
Hard-boiled egg
Creamy ranch and balsamic
vinaigrette

I like to think that one day, a chef in a kitchen somewhere, any-where (or *Everything, Everywhere, All at Once,* which was my favorite movie of 2022), needed a quick salad to serve, so she took all the things she had available at the time, put it in a bowl, and called it a chef salad.

Chef East and I, while we were working at Reed College in Portland, OR would take stainless steel bowls and tongs, walk out to the commons area where lunch was served for the students, and walk around to all the different stations and throw whatever we felt like into the bowl. Add a little lettuce and dressing and we had our own individual chef salads. And that was lunch.

CHICKEN SALAD

Chicken breast	Celery
Mayo	Salt
Pistachio	Pepper
Dried tart cherry	

- Use a rotisserie chicken, roasted chicken, or cook off chicken breast
- Mix diced or shredded chicken with all ingredients
- Season as needed

CHICKEN GORGONZOLA SALAD

Chicken breast	Red onion
Arugula	Toasted pecans or walnuts
Romaine	Gorgonzola cheese
Red leaf lettuce	White balsamic vinaigrette
Cherry tomato	

CHOPPED SALAD

Napa cabbage	Feta cheese
Red grapes	Dried cherries
Romaine	Pistachios
Cucumbers	Balsamic vinaigrette
Chickpeas	

CUCUMBER SALAD, JAPANESE STYLE

Cucumber	Salt
Soy sauce	Sugar
Rice vinegar	

Slice cucumber and toss with the rest of the ingredients. Think again about the 2:1 ratio with the soy sauce and the rice vinegar. Same with the sugar and salt. Adjust and taste as you perfect this side dish.

Refrigerate for 24 hours if possible.

CUCUMBER ONION SALAD

Cucumber	Salt
White onion	Sugar
White distilled vinegar	Water

Slice cucumber and onion and toss with the rest of the ingredients.

Let sit at least 24 hours if possible

My Grandma and Grandpa Walton (yes, I am a proud Walton!) had a huge garden back in the day. Many summer days were spent "tipping and tailing" green beans, and as a reward, Grandma would make this salad on a hot summer day from the cucumbers and onions in the garden.

It was one of my favorite memories of my childhood and remains a favorite treat.

I guess it was Grandma who taught me the first meaning of farm-to-table eating. And this was in the 1970s! Fresh vegetables, ohhhh, the fresh tomatoes. I didn't realize it then, but I do now, how different it is to grow your own food. There is nothing like a tomato freshly picked off the vine and popped right into your mouth.

I grow a garden of my own now, and I like to think I have Grandma to thank for my love of fresh vegetables, especially tomatoes.

Mom and I would eat a whole tomato, nicely sliced and salted, for our lunch most days in the summer. It was my favorite lunch, just the two of us.

FRUIT AND CHICKEN SALAD

Little gems lettuce
Chicken breast
Raspberry
Blueberry
Leek

Strawberry
Pineapple
Arugula
Marcona almonds
Balsamic vinaigrette

GRILLED BRUSSELS SPROUT AND AVOCADO SALAD

Brussels sprouts
Avocado
Salt

Pepper
Lemon vinaigrette

- Slice Brussels in half
- Brush with olive oil
- Season with salt and pepper
- Grill 6-8 minutes
- Dice avocado
- Toss together with vinaigrette

GRILLED CAESAR SALAD WITH GRILLED CROUTONS (yes, I said that)

Romaine
Sourdough bread
Parmesan cheese

Chef Tara's Spice Mix
Olive Oil
Chef Tara's Caesar Dressing

This is a fun take on the classic Caesar salad I experimented with when I had a hot grill going.

- Cut the romaine lettuce head in half
- Season with olive oil and Chef Tara's Spice Mix

- Place on the grill with the inside of the lettuce down on the grates
- Grill the lettuce about 2-3 minutes until the edges start to brown just a bit

For the croutons, you can either use the original crouton recipe in the book, OR you can "Chef it up." For this idea, we are doing just that.

- Take the sourdough loaf and cut it in half
- Generously add olive oil to both sides of the bread and season with Chef Tara's Spice Mix
- Lay the bread on the grill and cook about 3-4 minutes on both sides until nice and toasted
- Cut into cubes for the salad
- Make my Caesar dressing
- Toss all the ingredients together and serve on a nice platter

HONEYDEW SALAD

Burrata

Honeydew melon

Cucumber

Avocado

Sunflower seeds

Champagne vinaigrette

LEMON BRUSSELS SPROUT SALAD

Arugula

Shredded Brussels sprouts

Dried cranberry

Marcona almonds

Shaved parmesan

Lemon vinaigrette

MEDITERRANEAN BOWL

Ok, this might be one of my favorite things to discover. Have you ever seen those big green Farmers Fridge refrigerators in the airport concourses that just scream, "Eat me, I'm healthy"? This bowl comes from that refrigerator and it is glorious. I literally plan my arrival and departures around finding this green fridge at whatever airport I am in. I know exactly where it is at Chicago's Midway Airport. I wish I traveled more so I could enjoy it more often but instead, I recreated it for lunch one day. Thank you, Farmer's Fridge, for this inspiration!

Quinoa (white, black, and red)   Lemon juice
Garbanzo beans   Salt
Tomatoes   Pepper
Cucumbers   Cumin
Feta   Cinnamon
Spinach   All spice
Red onion   Lemon tahini dressing
Parsley

- Cook off the quinoa according to the instructions on the package and let cool
- Toss with diced tomatoes, cucumbers, and onions
- Add spinach, feta, and parsley
- Season with spices
- Toss with the lemon tahini dressing

NICOISE SALAD

Hard-boiled eggs
Green beans or haricot verts
Fingerling potatoes
Cherry tomatoes
Niçoise olives
Canned tuna
Mayo

Mustard
Sweet pickle relish
Salt
Pepper (or Chef Tara's
Spice Mix)
Red leaf lettuce
Red wine vinaigrette

This is one of my favorites because it has "all the things."

- Quick blanch the green beans
- Boil or roast off the potatoes
- Make a quick tuna salad
- Add all the things to a plate of lettuce and dress with the vinaigrette
- This salad makes a delicious meal.
- Modification:
- Use chicken breast or any other protein instead of the tuna salad
- Make a chicken salad
- Use sliced steak
- Add some salmon

ORANGE CRANBERRY SALAD

Arugula
Orange cuties
Raspberry
Dried cranberry
Pecan/candied ginger crumble
Balsamic vinaigrette

PANZANELLA OR BREAD SALAD

Sourdough bread
Olive oil
Chef Tara's Spice Mix
Tomato
Red onion
Cucumber
Balsamic vinaigrette

This is a giant crouton salad. Because my spice mix all began with making croutons for a Caesar salad, I took the croutons and made them larger to make this entree salad.

- Cut the bread into larger cubes
- Toss with spice mix and olive oil
- Bake at 350 degrees for 25-30 minutes
- Chunk the tomato
- Slice red onions
- Slice the cucumber into rounds and cut in half
- Make the balsamic vinaigrette
- Toss all the ingredients together
- Let it all set for at least 3-5 minutes, so the bread soaks up the vinaigrette for an amazing taste but keeps the croutons crunchy.

Modification:
Add sliced, grilled steak for a big steak salad
Ina Garten, in *Cook Like a Pro*, took the panzanella salad and combined it with a caprese salad for what she calls "The best of both worlds." She calls it a Tuscan Tomato and Bread Salad, and it's quite delightful.

PEPPER RAISIN SALAD

Little gems lettuce
Kiwi
Raisins
Red pepper
Yellow pepper

Orange cuties
Pepitas
Marcona almonds
Champagne vinaigrette

PINEAPPLE KIWI SALAD

Mixed greens
Blueberry
Raspberry
Peach
Pineapple

Kiwi
Blue cheese
Marcona almonds
Balsamic vinaigrette

RICE NOODLE COLD SALAD

Rice noodles (vermicelli)
Scallion
Red pepper
Radish

Red onion
Olive oil
Soba sauce

- Boil the noodles and blanch in cold water
- Toss with olive oil right away to prevent the noodles from sticking together
- Dice the onion and pepper
- Cut radishes by slicing into rounds then cut into matchstick strips
- Slice the scallions on the bias
- Toss with the soba salad dressing and lime juice

SALAD FOR A SANDO

Mixed greens
Red wine vinegar
Sugar
Oregano

Chiffonade mixed greens and toss with the rest of the ingredients for a sweet and tangy addition to any sandwich.

SNOW PEA SALAD

Shredded Brussels sprouts
Snow pea
Blueberry

Orange cuties
Orange pepper
White balsamic vinaigrette

SOBA NOODLE SALAD

Soba noodles
Carrot
Radish
Edamame

Spinach
Scallion
Soba sauce

- Boil noodles 4-5 minutes
- Strain
- Add to your bowl
- Top with fun, colorful vegetables
- Finish with sauce

STRAWBERRY PEAR SALAD

Strawberry
Pear
Mozzarella pearls
Basil
Balsamic vinaigrette

- Slice strawberries
- Dice pears
- Use mozzarella pearls as they are the perfect side for each bite
- Chiffonade basil to brighten the salad
- Toss with balsamic vinaigrette

SUMMER FRUIT SALAD

Arugula
Pear
Peach
Raspberry
Marcona almonds
Poppy vinaigrette

TACO SALAD

Ground beef
Taco seasoning
Lettuce
Tomato
Cheddar cheese
Guacamole
Sour cream
Scallion
Burrito-size flour tortilla
Olive oil
Chef Tara's Spice Mix
Hot sauce

I make these two or three days after we have done taco night with the leftover taco meat.

I already have all the things at the ready, so it makes a fun lunch and a house favorite.

The key is making the tortilla bowl. Once that is done, just start filling with all the taco fixings!

TORTELLINI SALAD

Cheese tortellini
Chicken breast
Radishes
Carrots
Scallions
Arugula
Lime soy vinaigrette

- Cook off tortellini
- Cook off chicken breast and dice
- Toss with the rest of the ingredients and the vinaigrette

TUNA SALAD

Albacore tuna in water, canned
Mayo
Yellow mustard
Sweet pickle relish (or dill if you prefer)
Salt
Pepper (or Chef Tara's Spice Mix)

Mix all ingredients together and call it a day.

Use it with crusty sourdough bread and mixed green lettuce for a great sando.

Add as a protein on the Niçoise Salad or to any of the entree salads.

When I first started making this, I noticed that the then four-year-old was very intrigued, and it became a much-requested lunch for her. By the time she was five, she was sitting at the island making it herself for her own lunch. She gathers all the ingredients and with many little spoons, she adds and mixes and tastes as she goes until she gets it just right. She doesn't need bread; she just eats it by the spoonful.

Even as a five-year-old, she doesn't need a recipe. She has the ingredients in front of her. Then she adds and tastes, adds and tastes, figuring it out as she goes, until finally, she has exactly what she is looking for in terms of a perfect tuna salad.

SIDE SALADS

Always keep some arugula on hand. It's a great green to make a simple side salad fancy.
Add whatever you have in the refrigerator or pantry.
Any fresh fruits
Dried fruits
Nuts
Shaved Parmesan

Have a vinaigrette on hand, either a balsamic vinaigrette or a poppy seed vinaigrette. In some instances, you can get away with just using a balsamic glaze.

CANTALOUPE SIDE SALAD

Cantaloupe
Feta cheese
Basil
Mint
Dried cherries
Arugula
Balsamic glaze

Think small.
Dice the cantaloupe into small cubes and toss with all the ingredients. It adds a bright, colorful side dish to any meal.

LEMON PARMESAN SIDE SALAD

Arugula
Shaved parmesan
Lemon vinaigrette

RASPBERRY PEAR SIDE SALAD

Arugula
Pear
Raspberry
Marcona almonds
Dried cranberries
Shaved parmesan
Poppy seed vinaigrette

CHAPTER 14

SANDOS (SANDWICHES)

"Do you like egg rolls? No, she doesn't eat meat pockets."

I LOVE A GOOD SANDWICH, A "SANDO" IN KITCHEN slang. But the key for me is the bread. If the bread sucks, you have ruined what could be great. I don't care how great the aioli is or that your bacon came from a prize-winning pig. There are a few joints that literally make their millions on just making a sandwich. But if the bread isn't good, then it's not worth your money. If you are going to make a sandwich, use great bread. Like sourdough. Then get your good stuff in the middle, give it a fun and fancy aioli or sauce it up, and have pride in what you are serving and eating.

Aioli is like a mayonnaise dressing. Although aioli and mayonnaise are both creamy emulsions, aioli is made from lemon juice, garlic, and olive oil while mayo is made from egg yolks and canola oil.

So, if you want to use mayo, then please do. Mix it with whatever your heart desires. Make a cranberry aioli for a turkey sandwich.

We have a great panini press, so oftentimes I'll take a simple sandwich, butter each side, and press it for lunch. Use fun breads like sourdough, ciabatta, and torta rolls. Make it a wrap with burrito-sized tortillas, adding hummus, guacamole, or an aioli as the base.

Grab some pita bread and create a gyro with regular lunch meats. Just layer turkey or chicken with red onions, tomatoes, cucumbers, some chickpeas, and top with some tzatziki sauce.

B'S FAVORITE SANDO

Turkey
Cucumber
Tomato

Salad for a Sando
Avocado mayo
Sourdough bread

- Make the salad for a sando
- Dice the avocado and mix with mayo to create a chunky creamy sauce
- Slice the tomatoes and cucumbers

CROQUE MONSIEUR

Thick sourdough bread
Ham
Gruyere, shredded

Bechamel sauce:
Roux: equal parts butter and flour
Milk
Chef Tara's Spice Mix

- Make the bechamel sauce by heating butter, adding flour, and whisking to create a paste
- Add milk to get a sauce consistency
- Season to taste
- Layer ham and Gruyere cheese in between the two bread slices
- Top with bechamel and more shredded Gruyere cheese
- Bake on a sheet pan in the oven at 375 degrees for about 15-20 minutes until the cheese starts to brown and bubble

I was in Paris many years ago and every day I would find a cafe and order this delightful sandwich. It's one of my favorite things and I encourage anyone going to Paris to order one of these. Or make your own!

Modification:
Add a fried egg on top and you have the Croque Madame.

FRIED GREEN TOMATO BLT

Green tomatoes
(un-ripened tomato)
Cornmeal
Salt
Bacon
Lettuce
Mayo
Sourdough bread

Ever since I saw the movie *Fried Green Tomatoes* with my friend Gina in 1991, I have been obsessed with these. I honestly think it's secretly the only reason I plant a garden every summer, so I can enjoy them whenever the tomatoes start to come in.

- Slice the tomatoes and season with salt
- Dredge in cornmeal
- Fry the bacon in a cast-iron skillet and set aside
- Fry the tomatoes in the bacon grease and let sit on a paper towel to soak up the grease
- Toast the sourdough bread
- Spread mayo on each side of the bread
- Layer bacon, lettuce, and tomatoes and enjoy

MUFFALETTA

Mortadella	Mozzarella
Ham	Olive tapenade
Salami	Really good bread
Provolone	

I met my college pals Holly and Jen at Mardi Gras 1994. Central Market in New Orleans made this sandwich famous. Of course, we had to have one. It was also the year I flew home, mostly hungover, with powdered sugar all over my face due to a bag of beignets from Cafe du Monde. But I digress…

This is a frequently requested sandwich from Alexis every year for her birthday, on a good crusty bread.

- Get all the meats and cheeses sliced
- Layer
- Layer
- Spread
- Spread
- Enjoy

If you can find a good tapenade, use that, otherwise make your own.

My Olive Tapenade:

In a blender, add:

- Kalamata olives, pitted
- Niçoise olives, pitted
- Peppadews
- Pickled carrots, celery, and cauliflower (Giardiniera)
- Pepperoncini

REUBEN SANDWICH

Corned beef	Rye bread
Swiss cheese	Thousand island dressing
Sauerkraut	

AVOCADO TOAST

Avocado toast is a favorite lunch option in the house. Since I was making it so often, I was able to come up with my guacamole recipe that I used for this:

- Avocados, 2-3
- A generous spoonful of Chef Tara's Spice Mix
- Squeeze of half a lime or lemon

Using a good sourdough bread or a nice whole grain wheat bread, I would create all kinds of different options for this lunch idea. Once I had the avocado spread down, the topping ideas were endless. From sweet to savory, it sometimes just came down to what I had on hand.

CAPRESE AVOCADO TOAST

Tomato
Basil
Mozzarella
Balsamic glaze

CARAMELIZED ONION AVOCADO TOAST

Strawberry
Caramelized onion
Blue cheese
Balsamic glaze

GREEK SALAD AVOCADO TOAST

Cucumbers
Red onion

Tomato
Feta cheese

PEAR KIWI AVOCADO TOAST

Pear
Strawberry
Kiwi

Blue cheese
Alfalfa sprouts
Balsamic glaze

SMOKED SALMON AVOCADO TOAST

Smoked salmon
Pear

Blue cheese
Balsamic glaze

STRAWBERRY BURRATA AVOCADO TOAST

Burrata
Strawberries

Spiced nuts and candied ginger
Honey balsamic glaze

STRAWBERRY PEACH AVOCADO TOAST

Peach
Strawberry
Feta
Pecan/candied ginger crumble
Balsamic glaze

CHAPTER 15

SAUCES

"Looks like you're not wearing that shirt, fancy pants."

"SAUCES ARE OFTEN CONSIDERED ONE OF THE greatest tests of a chef's skill. The successful pairing of a sauce with food demonstrates technical expertise, an understanding of the food, and the ability to judge and evaluate a dish's flavors, textures and colors" (*The Professional Chef*, pg. 355).

This is where testing your flavor profile comes into play again. A sauce can make or break a dish.

When I went to culinary school, sauces were one of my favorite sections of learning. We had to perfect the "Mother Sauces" of the great Auguste Escoffier. So, as I went to describe this section, I thought of the Escoffier website and found this perfect blog entry from March 2020 that really explains it all so well, so I am adding it here verbatim:

> He didn't realize it when he published them, but Auguste Escoffier left a lifelong culinary legacy when he created the five "mother sauces."
>
> They are the basis for virtually every sauce used in modern cuisine...and if you're attending culinary school, you're sure to learn them as a foundation for your education.

From alfredo to bourguignonne, demi-glace to cheddar cheese, you'll discover that one of the five mother sauces is the base in hundreds of unique sauce recipes. Understanding their origins, their composition, and how to master them should be a priority for anyone studying culinary arts.

Some critics claim that the mother sauces are "outdated"…but the humble pasta sauce and gravy wouldn't exist were it not for this foundation…not to mention the myriad delicious creations that begin with these building blocks.

Here is a brief tour of the five mother sauces…

HOLLANDAISE SAUCE

Probably the most well-known of the mother sauces, it's a household name in restaurants, where it's served with Eggs Benedict—an American creation that's known for its rich, creamy, calorie-loaded character.

Eggs, butter, and lemon form the basis for this versatile sauce that goes beyond the breakfast and brunch table. It's been poured over grilled and steamed vegetables like asparagus, artichokes, and broccoli, and kept as a side dipping sauce for a range of dishes.

One of the most popular variations is Bearnaise—one of the sister sauces that also includes Sauce Mousseline, Sauce Noisette, Sauce Dijon, and Sauce Maltaise.

Hollandaise is a delicious, rich addition to many dishes, but it can be finicky to prepare. Temperature and technique play big roles in the making of a smooth, creamy Hollandaise, so it's not very common in everyday cooking.

BECHAMEL SAUCE

The white sauce of the family, béchamel is a flavor overload that begins with flour, butter, and milk…the seasoning is up to the individual chef.

The French usually keep it very simple—a little salt and pepper—while the Italian version often includes a little nutmeg. Many chefs will steep the milk with a bay leaf and a whole onion that's been studded with a couple of cloves, giving the milk a rich flavor before it's combined with the roux.

However you choose to flavor béchamel, it will be the basis for nearly every butter or cream-based sauce you're preparing. Even a simple mac 'n cheese begins with this base!

While Chef Escoffier didn't invent this recipe, his interpretation of this mother sauce is considered the culinary authority.

VELOUTÉ SAUCE

This silky, blonde mother sauce shares some common traits with béchamel, but instead of adding milk to the roux, a clear stock is added. The velouté sauce has a pale blonde color because the bones aren't roasted before creating the stock.

Any bones can be used—fish, veal, beef, poultry—as a stock base for velouté, just as long as they aren't roasted, as this darkens the stock and changes the flavor profile.

Once you have the base, a variety of ingredients can be added…wine, cream, flavored juices. The only limit is your imagination with this versatile sauce.

TOMATO SAUCE

Sure, we know it as "pasta sauce" but a good tomato sauce base can do so much more. Traditionally it's seasoned with oregano and basil, onions and garlic, cayenne and coriander, and suits a range of dish—rice, pasta, fish, poultry, pork, beef, potatoes—you get the idea.

Escoffier's traditional "sauce tomate" begins with salted pork belly, onion, bay leaves, thyme, puréed or fresh tomatoes, roux, garlic, salt, sugar, and pepper. If that looks too ambitious—or you're following specific dietary restrictions—you can leave out the pork belly and the roux and make a basic tomato sauce.

This sauce may be a little out of date, but it's still a delicious foundation for tomato-based recipes.

ESPAGNOLE (SPANISH) SAUCE

Believe it or not, this sauce has nothing to do with Spanish cuisine, per se. As the story goes, King Louis XIII's bride, Anne—a Spanish princess—had Spanish cooks who insisted on putting tomatoes in the basic brown sauce to give it a more well-rounded flavor. The sauce was a smash hit and named after their country.

Unlike the other mother sauces, Espagnole has very strong flavors and is usually diluted with another sauce or broth—it's rarely served on its own. The rich, distinct flavor comes from roasted veal bone broth, rather than beef, setting it apart from its milder mother sauces.

You'll find Espagnole sauce at the base of favorites like sauce bourguignonne, mushroom sauce, and a creole-inspired sauce Africaine.

Whether you're an amateur cook in your home kitchen or studying at a culinary school to further your career in the industry, having a mastery of these five mother sauces will elevate your cooking. They form the foundation for so many creative—and traditional—dishes, and they're yours to explore. – Escoffieronline.com Auguste Escoffier

By starting with each of the mother sauces, your options are limitless.

From Bechamel:

- Add cream and lemon for a basic cream sauce
- Add cheese, Worcestershire, and mustard for the Cheddar Sauce

- Add Gruyere, butter, and cream to make the Mornay Sauce
- Add cream, butter, paprika, and diced shellfish for the Nantua Sauce
- Add diced onions that have been sweated to make the Soubise Sauce

From Velouté:

- Add fish stock, shallots, white wine, and butter to get a Bercy Sauce
- Add Veal Stock, egg yolk, cream, and lemon to get an Allemande Sauce
- Add Chicken stock, mushrooms, and cream to get the Supreme Sauce
- Take the Allemande Sauce and add tomato paste and butter to get an Aurora Sauce
- Add fish stock, cream, cayenne, and lobster to get the Cardinal Sauce

From Espagnole:

- Add mushrooms, shallots, white wine, and tomatoes for the Chasseur Sauce
- Add white wine, shallots, lemons, and tarragon to get the Chateaubriand Sauce
- Add red wine, shallots, bay leaf, and thyme to get a Bordelaise Sauce
- Add onion, mustard, sugar, and butter for the Robert Sauce
- Add onion, mushrooms, white wine, and tomato for the Duxelles Sauce

From Tomato:

- Add onions, celery, garlic, pepper, thyme, and cayenne for the Creole Sauce
- Take the Creole Sauce and add mushrooms and olives for the Spanish Sauce

- Add mushrooms, butter, and ham for the Milanaise Sauce
- Add garlic, olives, anchovy, and capers for the Neapolitan Sauce
- Add mirepoix (carrots, celery, onion), ground meat, red wine, and oregano for a classic Bolognese Sauce

From Hollandaise:

- Add shallots, tarragon, and reduced vinegar to get a Bearnaise Sauce
- Add whipped cream for the Mousseline Sauce
- Add orange juice and orange zest for the Maltaise Sauce
- Add saffron to get the Grimrod Sauce
- From the Bearnaise Sauce, add tomato paste and heavy cream for the Choron Sauce

Mix all the things little by little until you create your own perfect sauce.

Take notes.

What works? What doesn't?

Too salty? Less soy.

Too spicy? Less sriracha.

SOY VS SHOYU VS TAMARI

Shoyu is the Japanese word for soy sauce. When you see shoyu, it's just soy sauce.

What is soy sauce?
Soy sauce is a condiment made from a mix of fermented soybeans, water, salt, and a grain, such as wheat or rice. There are different types of soy sauce, including Chinese, Japanese, Korean, Taiwanese, and Indonesian. Its color and flavor profile—sweet, salty, a little funky—varies depending on where it's made and how long it's aged.

What is tamari?

Tamari is a gluten-free Japanese sauce made by pressing the liquid from miso, a fermented soybean paste of soybeans, water, salt, and koji (fermented rice). Tamari has a thick viscosity, is dark brown in color, and has a rich, savory flavor rounded out with a subtle sweetness. Because it does not contain any wheat, tamari is gluten-free.

ALFREDO

Stick butter
Garlic
Heavy cream

Parmesan
Chef Tara's Spice Mix

BANG BANG SAUCE

Mayonnaise
Sriracha

Thai chili sauce
Rice vinegar

BBQ SAUCE

Ketchup
Brown sugar
Apple cider vinegar
Molasses

Water
Mustard powder
Chef Tara's Spice Mix

BROCCOLI BEEF COOKING SAUCE

Chicken stock
Rice wine vinegar

Oyster sauce
Cornstarch

BROCCOLI BEEF MARINADE

Soy sauce
Sesame oil
Cornstarch

BROWN BUTTER SAGE SAUCE

Butter
Sage
Salt

Melt the butter in a skillet or pan and add the sage leaves and some salt. Let it cook down until the butter turns a medium-brown color being careful not to let it burn. Should take a few minutes but watch the pot as it can quickly go from brown butter to burnt butter in a second.

BUFFALO SAUCE

Frank's Red Hot
Butter

Heat sauce up in a pot and add butter to finish. Toss with grilled, baked or air-fried wings and enjoy!

CARIBBEAN JERK SAUCE

For the jerk sauce, combine the following in a blender and puree into sauce form:

Soy sauce
Onion
Thyme
Scallions
Garlic cloves
All spice
Salt

Sugar
Nutmeg
Cinnamon
Pepper
Lemon juice
Canola oil

CHEF TARA'S EVERYDAY ASIAN SAUCE

Soy sauce
Mirin

Hoisin
Rice wine vinegar

I use equal parts of all four of these that I shake up in a Ball jar and keep on hand each week.

CHEF TARA'S SPECIAL SAUCE

Mayo
Yellow mustard
Ketchup

Sweet or dill relish
Chef Tara's Spice Mix

CHIMICHURRI

Parsley

Red wine vinegar

Garlic

Shallot

Oregano

Lemon juice

Olive oil

Salt

Pepper

Combine all the ingredients in a blender and puree until nice and smooth
Use as a garnish for steak, chicken, and seafood.

CREAMY TOMATO SAUCE

Marinara

Heavy cream

DRUNKEN NOODLE SAUCE

Oyster sauce

Soy sauce

Sugar

Water

ENCHILADA SAUCE

Olive oil

Flour

Chili powder

Cumin

Oregano

Beef stock

Tomato sauce

Make a roux with the oil and flour
    Add the spices, stock, and tomato sauce to create the thickness you desire

You can make this gluten-free by using cornstarch as a slurry at the end to make the sauce thicker. Play around with it and add more heat if you desire. You can also use vegetable or chicken stock.

KOREAN SHORT RIBS MARINADE

Onion	Gochujang
Garlic	Sesame oil
Ginger	Pear
Soy sauce	Kiwi
Brown sugar	Orange juice
Rice vinegar	7-Up

LEMON PARMESAN SAUCE

Melted butter	Lemon juice
Garlic	Salt
Parmesan cheese	Pepper

LETTUCE WRAP COOKING SAUCE

Soy sauce	Oyster sauce
Mirin	Rice vinegar

LETTUCE WRAP DIPPING SAUCE

Sugar	Chives
Water	Hot mustard
Soy sauce	Sriracha
Rice vinegar	Chili oil finish

MARINARA

Tomatoes
Garlic
Olive oil

Salt
Pepper

MISO GLAZE

Miso
Mirin/sake
Brown sugar

Minced ginger
Soy sauce
Toasted sesame oil

ORANGE CHICKEN SAUCE

Orange juice
Soy sauce
Rice vinegar

Sugar
Cornstarch
Water

Add orange juice, soy sauce, rice vinegar and sugar to a pot and bring it to a boil, then let it simmer. Make a "slurry" out of cornstarch and water and slowly add this to the pot, whisking as you pour, to create a thicker, saucier consistency.

PAD THAI SAUCE

Brown sugar
Fish sauce

Tamarind
Oyster sauce

PEANUT SAUCE

Coconut milk
Peanut butter
Soy sauce
Rice vinegar
Sambal oelek or Lahtt sauce

Honey
Garlic clove
Ginger
Lime juice
Hot water

POKE SAUCE

Soy sauce
Rice vinegar

Sesame oil
Hoisin

REMOULADE

Mayo
Dijon
Lemon
Parsley

Garlic
Paprika
Chef Tara's Spice Mix

SOBA NOODLE BOWL SAUCE

Rice vinegar
Soy sauce

Oyster sauce
Sesame oil

TARTAR SAUCE

Mayo
Dill pickle relish
Fresh Dill
Capers

Chives
Lemon juice
Worcestershire sauce

TOMATO MEAT SAUCE

Marinara
Ground beef

TZATZIKI

Greek yogurt
Shredded cucumber
Minced garlic

Lemon juice
Fresh dill
Chef Tara's Spice Mix

CHAPTER 16

VINAIGRETTES/DRESSINGS

"They are very small but very impressive."

BALSAMIC
VINAIGRETTE

OIL

DIJON

HONEY

VINEGAR

"VINAIGRETTES ARE THOUGHT OF MAINLY AS DRESS-ings for green salads, but they are used in many other ways as well: as marinades for grilled or broiled foods; to dress salads made from pastas, grains, vegetables, and beans; as dips; as sauces served with hot or cold entrees and appetizers; or brushed on sandwiches.

"A standard vinaigrette ratio of three parts oil to one part acid works well as a starting point, but the vinaigrette needs to be tasted and evaluated whenever a change is made in the type of oil, acid, or specific flavoring ingredient" (*The Professional Chef*).

While the 3:1 ratio is the standard starting point, I typically lean more toward 2:1 oil to vinegar as I like my vinaigrettes a bit tangier in taste.

A house-made vinaigrette will last about two weeks, whereas dairy based dressings will last up to a week.

ASIAN LIME VINAIGRETTE

Soy sauce
Lime juice
Sherry vinegar
Ginger minced

Sugar
Maple syrup
Sriracha
Toasted sesame oil

ASIAN SLAW DRESSING

Ginger, minced
Mayo
Dijon
Soy sauce

Rice vinegar
Honey
Sesame oil

B'S FAVORITE VINAIGRETTE

Lime
Soy sauce
Dijon

Rice vinegar
Sugar
Toasted sesame oil

BASIL VINAIGRETTE

Basil
Honey
Dijon mustard

Rice vinegar
Grapeseed oil

BLUE CHEESE DRESSING

Mayo	Blue cheese
Sour cream	Chives
Lemon juice	Sriracha

(You can also make ranch dressing and add blue cheese as a quick option.)

BUTTERMILK RANCH

Buttermilk	Worcestershire sauce
Mayo	Fresh dill
Sour cream	Fresh parsley
Apple cider vinegar	Chef Tara's Spice Mix

CHEF TARA'S CAESAR DRESSING

Mayo	Red wine vinegar
Dijon	Worcestershire sauce
Lemon juice	Parmesan cheese
Garlic	Chef Tara's Spice Mix

COLESLAW DRESSING

Mayo	Poppy seed
Rice vinegar	Celery seed
Honey	Celery salt

CITRUS HERB VINAIGRETTE

Lemon juice
Lime
Orange
Parsley
Honey

Shallot
Garlic
Chef Tara's Spice Mix
Grapeseed oil

CLASSIC BALSAMIC VINAIGRETTE

Balsamic vinegar
Dijon

Honey
Grapeseed oil

FRENCH DRESSING

Sugar
Ketchup
White vinegar
Celery seed

Chili powder
Dry mustard
Chef Tara's Spice Mix
Grapeseed oil

GINGER BALSAMIC VINAIGRETTE

White balsamic vinegar
Ginger, minced

Honey
Grapeseed oil

EVERYDAY ASIAN VINAIGRETTE

Rice vinegar
Soy sauce

Honey
Toasted sesame oil

EVERYDAY RED WINE VINAIGRETTE

Red wine vinegar   Oregano
Sugar   Grapeseed oil
Chef Tara's Spice Mix

LEMON VINAIGRETTE

Lemon juice   Chef Tara's Spice Mix
Champagne vinegar   Grapeseed oil

LEMON TAHINI DRESSING

Whole lemon juice   Salt
Tahini   Pepper
Water   Grapeseed oil
Garlic

LIME SOY VINAIGRETTE

Lime juice   Apple cider vinegar
Soy sauce   Sesame oil
Sugar

MISO VINAIGRETTE

Miso   Rice vinegar
Honey   Ginger
Dijon   Grapeseed oil

MIGNONETTE

Champagne vinegar or rice vinegar
Shallot

Fresh parsley
*Cilantro or jalapeno optional

ORANGE SESAME BALSMIC VINAIGRETTE

Orange juice
Balsamic vinegar
Ginger
Dijon mustard

Salt
Pepper
Sesame oil

ORANGE VINAIGRETTE

Orange marmalade
Champagne vinegar

Honey
Grapeseed oil

PEANUT VINAIGRETTE

Garlic
Ginger
Tamari
Brown sugar

Peanuts
Champagne vinegar
Sesame oil

POPPY SEED VINAIGRETTE

Apple cider vinegar
Sugar
Honey

Poppy seeds
Grapeseed oil

RUSSIAN DRESSING

Mayo	Lemon juice
Sweet relish	Horseradish
Ketchup	Worcestershire sauce

SESAME LIME VINAIGRETTE

Lime	Rice vinegar
Ginger	Maple syrup
Soy sauce	Sesame oil

SICHUAN VINAIGRETTE

Garlic	Soy sauce
Ginger	Sherry vinegar
Tahini	Honey
Peanut butter	Chili oil
Sherry	Sesame oil

THAI VINAIGRETTE

Lime juice	Brown sugar
Rice vinegar	Mint
Fish sauce	Peanut oil/sesame oil
Jalapeno	

TOMATO BASIL VINAIGRETTE

Basil
Sun-dried tomato
Balsamic vinegar
Red wine vinegar

Maple syrup
Dijon
Grapeseed oil

WHITE BALSAMIC VINAIGRETTE

White balsamic vinegar
Apple cider vinegar
Honey
Apple juice

Garlic powder
Onion powder
Ginger
Olive oil

EPILOGUE

This manuscript has been a lifelong dream of mine. I have been a "writer" my whole life, keeping journals and chronicling my adventures with my Seester in our garage in an old book I used as my "detective log." That book is still on my bookshelf, my younger self detailing the goings-on in our house in child-like penmanship with a pencil.

This adventure began in 2021. I think I had an idea in my mind back then to take meticulous notes of the days in the kitchen in my Moleskine, and that maybe one day down the road it would/could finally result in my dream of being a published author coming to fruition.

I wish you could see the actual journal itself. It's pretty cool. I have shown you some of the pages but imagine a whole year full of ideas in a book.

Now here we are in 2025 and she's done and in your hands. I hope you can feel all my love and passion for cooking and what I do as you go through this book and make these dishes your own. This is my labor of love and my gift to you.

I ended up cooking for the family for nearly three years and what fun we had. We all became such good friends and they continue to support me even today. B and I still have our little book club and share our favorite reads. I still go to soccer games the little ones are participating in.

Lately, I have been volunteering at Navarro Farm here in Frankfort, IL, teaching culinary to the "Farmers." Navarro Farm is a special place. The Navarro family five-acre farm has one purpose:

to create a place for individuals with special needs (the "Farmers") to participate in an agricultural experience with the hopes of increasing their social skills and independence (<u>Navarrofarm. org</u>). The joy this place brings me is second to none and it soothes my soul every time I am there working with the Farmers. For the upcoming 2025 season, I'll be the culinary program director, bringing even more fun and flavor to the farm.

In January of 2024, I wrote down three things I wanted to manifest in the coming year: *The Today Show*, the Food Network, and Oprah's Favorite Things. Two of the three fun dreams came true in June of 2024. My spice mix was featured on *The Today Show* and my business was part of a wonderful article written by Joey Skladany for Food Network. Both focused on PRIDE and gay-owned businesses to support in the coming year. I was over the moon!

Also in 2024, I launched five new varieties of Chef Tara's Spice Mix. The original spice mix has been so well-received and because it is used on literally everything, what I did was use that as the base and added three or four new ingredients to it to create the five new mixes: Dad's Chili, Seester's Steak, Taco, Herb, and BBQ. I was able to participate in the Frankfort Farmer's Market for the summer and fall sessions and everything sold very well. Once people taste it, they understand just how good everything is. These are all seasonings that I use throughout my daily cooking chores.

I have had two more CRPS surgeries. In March 2023, my neurosurgeon in Chicago replaced the battery/implant in my abdomen that had been working since the initial surgery in 2014. Then on Halloween 2024, they went in and replaced the wires that lead from the paddle on my spine to the implant in the abdomen. This gave me a lot of down time to recover and finalize this book. It's a constant struggle to remain pain free, which doesn't exist in my world, but this device does help minimize it somewhat and enables me to continue moving forward. I do not rely on pain pills to get by, I just keep pushing through, one foot in front of the other, so I can realize my dreams.

CITATIONS AND IDEAS

Culinary Institute of America, The. *The Professional Chef*. John Wiley & Sons, Inc., 2006

Dornenburg, Andrew and Karen Page. *Culinary Artistry*. John Wiley & Sons, Inc., 1996.

Escoffier, Auguste. "Mother Sauces". *Escoffieronline.com,* 6 October 2022.

Garten, Ina. *Cook Like A Pro*. Clarkson Potter, 2018

Garten, Ina. *Go-To Dinners: A Barefoot Contessa Cookbook*. Clarkson Potter, 2022

Hesser, Amanda. *The Essential New York Times Cookbook*. W.W. Norton & Company, Inc., 2021.

Medtronic. "Spinal cord stimulation for chronic pain". *Medtronic.com,* 6 October 2022.

Nosrat, Samin. *Salt, Fat, Acid, Heat*. Simon & Schuster, 2017.

Seguit, Niki. *The Flavor Thesaurus: A Compendium of Pairings. Recipes and Ideas for the Creative Cook*. Bloomberg USA, 2010.

Sifton, Sam. *No-Recipe Recipes*. Tenspeed Press, 2021.

IDEAS

Abraham, Lena. Tuna Poke, Best Poke Bowls, Delish

AJ's Lena-Maid Meats, The Butcher

Bepe & Gianni's Restaurant, Eugene, OR

Beria, Albert. Spain on a Fork

Biegel, Katie Lee. BBQ Ribs, Food Network

Binkowski, Shawna. Pineapple Fried Rice

Bittman, Mark. Chicken Curry, NYT Cooking App

Bittman, Mark. Paella, NYT Cooking

Bon Appetit Test Kitchen

Brown, Alton. Corned Beef, Food Network

Brown, Alton. Shepherd's Pie, Food Network Test Kitchen

Burke, Susan and Stacey. Baked Spaghetti

Changs, P.F. Chicken Lettuce Wraps

Cheesecake Factory, salad

Child, Julia. Boeuf Bourguignon, *Mastering the Art of French Cooking*, 1961

Chongchitnant, Palin. Chicken Satay, Hot Thai Kitchen

CHOP: Children's Hospital of Philadelphia, "What is FPIES?"

Choy, Roy. Korean Short Ribs, Masterclass

Cochran, Jenifer. Spatchcock chicken

Cooking For My Soul. Huli Huli

Custom Seafood

Denang, Chef. Pad Thai

DiGregorio, Sarah. Lemony Greek Chicken, Spinach and Potato Stew, NYT Cooking App

Dolan, Maggie. Mulligatawny, Lobster Roll

Drummond, Ree. Apple sauce, Baked Ziti, The Pioneer Woman

Drummond, Ree. Enchiladas, Food Network

Florence, Tyler. Peanut Sauce, Food Network

Fontana Forni. Roasted Chicken

Forkish, Ken. Flour, Water, Salt, Yeast, 2012

Franklin, Aaron and Jordan Mackay. *Franklin Barbecue: A Meat Smoking Manifesto*, 2015

French, Erin. Potato Salad, *The Lost Kitchen*, 2017

Giantsofsiam.com

Harris, Scott. Caprese Pasta, Francesca's Restaurant

Hayward, Sam. Lobster Roll, Food and Wine

Heck, Mary-Francis. Lobster Roll, Food and Wine

Herrling, Marnie. Mom's Broccoli Cheddar Casserole, Mom's Potato Salad

Hog Island Oyster Company. Oysters, clams, mussels

Hoogenhyde, Chef Patrick. Halibut, Leek and Mushroom, Bridge Seafood Restaurant, Anchorage, AK

Khoury-Harold, Layla. "Soy v Tamari", Food Network Kitchen, Jan. 31, 2023

Leung, Bill, Judy, Sarah, and Kaitlin. The Woks of Life

Lopez-Alt, J. Kenji. *The Wok: Recipes and Techniques*, 2021

Lopez-Alt, J. Kenji. *The Food Lab*, 2015

Lui, Vivian. *Eat California: Vibrant Recipes from the West Coast*, 2020

Miyashiro, Lauren. Fish Tacos, Delish

O'Neil, Molly. Teriyaki Chicken, NYT Cooking

Onohawaiianrecipes.com

Ott's Tavern. Cod Fish Fry

Packard, Dan and Debbie. The Cow

Panera Bread Company. Salad

Pham, Charles. *Vietnamese Home Cooking*, 2012

Pham, Charles. Shaking Beef, *The Slanted Door: Modern Vietnamese Food*, 2014

Powell, Julie. Boeuf Bourguignon, Julie and Julia, 2009

Professional Chef, The. Vinaigrettes,

Saffitz, Claire. Pad Thai, Bon Appetit

Segal, Jenn. Pot pie, Once Upon a Chef

Sharma, Amandeep. Butter Chicken, Adapted by Sam Sifton, NYT Cooking App

Shulman, Martha Rose. Stir-Fried Garlic Green Beans, NYT Cooking

Sifton, Sam. Glazed Ham, NYT Cooking App

Singleton Hachisu, Nancy. *Japan: The Cookbook*, 2018

Stewart, Martha. Spatchcock chicken

The Tiki Terrace. Loco Moco,

Theoktisto, Anna. Short rib rage, Food and Wine

Today Show

Triefenbach, Cheryl. all things Mom

Triefenbach, Lee. Dad's Chili

Viola, Lisa. Sloppy Joe

Walton, Marvene

Webrestaurantstore. Mise en Place

Wei, Clarissa. "What is Rice Vinegar," Food Network Kitchen, July
    25, 2023,
Weibel, Alexa. Chicken Milanese, NYT Cooking App
Xie, June. Pork Adobo, Delish
Xie, June. Chicken Satay, Delish
Zhu, Maggie. Broccoli Beef, Omnivores Cookbook
Zimmern, Andrew. Crab Cakes, Food and Wine

MANY THANKS

This book would not be possible without the opportunity to cook for the amazing family who opened their house and kitchen to me in 2021 and trusted me with feeding their family and the girls. I am forever grateful. You know who you are.

To Dalita for that first phone call that changed everything.

To my FAMILY: Dad, Seester, Erik, Sydney, and Camryn, and of course Mom who is looking down with pride as her daughter has an ISBN and a book out. She was the first one that taught me to love reading and writing and embrace books of all kinds. Dad and Seester lent their names and thoughts to their own spice mixes. Your support has been unwavering, and I love you all immensely. Sydney and Camryn, you are my favorite humans and I am so incredibly proud of you both for being exactly who you are. Dream big my loves. Aunt Tara will always have your back.

To my Frannie Pack: Carri, Deb, Holly, Janene, Jenifer, Kendall, Shannon: our yearly beach trips to Long Beach recharge my soul and warm my heart. The friendship, chats, and laugh-till-you pee hilarity that ensues can't be taken for granted. Meredith Grey had her person, I have my people. I am forever grateful and appreciative to all of you for everything.

To Sue, Stacey, Alexis, Brandon, Paige, and Cade—you have played a fun part in allowing me to play with food over the last ten years since moving back to Illinois. I love our weekly family dinners! Brandon, thanks for telling me to bottle the crouton spice mix.

To Angie Eckert, my friend since high school, THANK YOU for believing in me and my products and being the first to sell them. You have been an invaluable resource the last few years and I appreciate and love you dearly.

To Caroline Foglton Shanahan, my partner-in-crime, for assisting me the last few years with all things spice mix. From bottling to social media to helping at the Farmer's Market, your help has been invaluable. Here's to much more fun in the future, my friend.

To Lisa, who put up with me during culinary school and Tara B., who was my first inspiration for all things culinary and finding out where my passion could possibly take me.

To all my culinary instructors at Le Cordon Bleu: Portland, THANK YOU for educating me.

To the Navarro family, thank you for letting me be a part of your world. Carter, you make a great sous chef by my side! The Farm has enriched my life more than I could begin to explain. All the Farmers have taught me to live every day to the fullest. They embrace life with such joy that you can't help but smile. I appreciate you all.

To Kate Mueller for her original artwork for my spice mix label and Colleen and John Mueller for allowing me to use the island to build my website and labels with the extraordinary Michelle Maurer, and for being my very first order! Thank you for your love and friendship all these years and our many outings at Wrigley Field for Cardinals vs. Cubs games. Hi Jack and O!

Special thanks to Chef Crista Luedtke, Chef Sean Andrade, and Chef Wendy Bennett for their endorsements of the book. Thanks for letting me pick your brain when I needed some advice.

To my superhero Joey Skladany, for taking a chance on me and my spice mixes, and for featuring me in your article, then presenting them proudly on *The Today Show!* What a dream that was. I am so very thankful for you.

When I first started this project, I texted one person, Stephanie Chandler, my publisher. We had worked together for years at Veritas back in the day, and when I left to pursue my passion, she did the same and opened a bookstore. From there, her love of books led her to starting Authority Publishing in California. Stephanie became my mentor on this project, guiding me with her expertise from start to finish. My editor Amberly Finarelli has held my hand through the process over numerous zooms and emails back and forth. Thank you both and to the whole staff at Authority Publishing for your assistance in making my dream come true.

2/7/22   Week 41   O: 7:10 P:
          Ideas   D: 7/6 4-2

F Pulled Pork - Keto style   Steak Salad
~~Dumplings / Banh w/ lettu~~   Cheesecake Chop
M Shrimp Tacos - Mango Salsa - Pineapple
TH Roast Chx w/pot, carrots x2
W Steak w/ Bread Salad 4B3   Freezer
T Pineapple Fried Rice / chx   X Steaks.
                                      X Chx - whole
X Liquid Eggs   X yogurt   X Pork Butt
X Olive Oil   X straw   X Chx Thigh?
X Wild granola   X blue
  Puff pastry   X veg
X Pork Crack/wings A mango
  Italian bread   X pineapple
X Garlic - peeled X mandarins Sliced.
X arugula   X Snow peas
X red pepp X orange X chicken breast
X jalapeño   X Cherry tomes
X red onion   bun
X cilantro   fridge
X Shrimp   Pillsbury - pizza
X taco shells soft French Bread
X Avocado   Pizza Dough
X Carrots   Cucumber
X potatoes - fingerling ✓
X ground pork
  olives
  Round dumpling wrappers
  Bamboo Sticks ?
X wonton strips
  bean sprouts
  Plum Sauce

MON   XW - who's around?
X Chopped Chx Salad x 2   X Lunch: Veg Wrap: B   TH?
X Plum Ses Dressing   X Steak Salad - d
X Omelet   X T - Dinner
  Parfaits   X Eggs   X Cashews
X Mango Salsa   X Pineapple X rice
X - red pep   X Red Pep X Soy
  - jalapeño   X green onion X chili garlic
  - lime   X garlic
  - onion
  - cilantro   WED
X Cuke   X Prep chicken
X make chips   X Fire @ 4:30 - 6:00 4/25
X Cook off chicken   X potatoes
X prep orange   X Carrots
X Fry Rice Noodles   X make omelets - veg wrap
  Saute Shrimp   X Prep TH ① ? nos
                                  X Prep Pork Butt - day onw
TUE   X Make BBQ sauce
X Soba Bowl - B   X Tzatiki
X Chx Bowl - J   X Veg Wrap
X Edamame   pea
  Cauliflower   TH
X Cabbage Asian sauce   X BBQue chx salad - lunch
X Scallion   X Cook off 2nd chicken X
X carrots   X Cube bread
  Ginger Plum Dressing   X make balsamic/dressing
X Pineapple   ① veg side? - saute veg
X broccoli   X make vert - Dill
                                  ② Cole slaw
X Parfaits x 5   SEAR RIBEYES
                                  X Chunk cuke
                                  X Toss Salad - Panzanella